NOT UNTO DEATH

A True life Story

David Ade Fadipe

Grosvenor House
Publishing Limited

This book is published by
Grosvenor House Publishing Ltd
Link House
140 The Broadway, Tolworth, Surrey, KT6 7HT.
www.grosvenorhousepublishing.co.uk

A CIP record for this book
is available from the British Library

ISBN 978-1-83975-555-2

TABLE OF CONTENTS

ENDORSEMENTS

"Thank you so much for a very inspiring book. I am very encouraged by the contents and structure of the writing in this book, and it will go a long way to help so many others going through similar difficult situations with their health."

Dr Benjamin Ayo Adeyemi
Consultant Clinical Cardiology
The Royal Marsden NHS Foundation Trust – RPY

I would like to use this opportunity to give thanks to our Almighty God on your behalf and thank the Lord for your better half during your trials and tribulations up till now. You have an incredibly supportive wife and daughter, and we bless God for them. It is commendable and noble of you to share your story and take us through your traumatic journey with leukaemia. I was a witness to both times in your life when you were afflicted by this terrible illness. Toyin and I observed at a close range how it toiled on your well-being emotionally, mentally, physically, and spiritually during our many visits to you at the hospital. We usually chatted, talked, prayed, laughed, and even cried. But one thing always stood out about you, you always to remain positive and have the desire to live and a strong will to overcome this thing called cancer. In all things, we must learn to always give thanks to God. Prayer works, divine miracles happen, and, in your situation, you should realise that your case is a miracle to all, you were given a third chance at life, most people only had one, please use it to help heal the afflicted, the sick and others. We hope and pray that this book of your experiences is a blessing to the reader and to the community at large. To God be the glory.

Akin and Toyin Seweje

David Fadipe is a survivor, someone who is always grateful regardless of the circumstances. I believe this mindset and his faith in God contributed to his victory over cancer. I believe everything worked together for him; physically, medically, spiritually, and mentally. I am happy he is alive to tell his story, to appreciate God's goodness and to encourage others and give them hope.

I believe you will be encouraged to have faith as you read about his journey in this book. You will be inspired to believe you can overcome cancer or any other seemingly impossible situation.

Tunde Omopariola

EPILOGUE

"Many believe that God sometimes heals the sick, but they have no personal knowledge of Jesus as our indwelling healer. They know nothing about the many facts which prove that physical health is part of Salvation," T L Osborn – One Hundred Divine Healing Facts.

This book is about the story of my experience with Acute Myeloid Leukaemia (AML), a blood related cancer twice in ten years and how God healed me on both occasions. Through the leading of the Holy Spirit, I have kept the narrative as simple as possible. The title '*Not unto Death*' is based on the scripture that I held unto following the diagnosis in 2005. The title serves as a catalyst in writing the story of my life and my battle with Leukaemia cancer, pre-diagnoses, during and after treatment, relapse and remission periods. I was in two minds whom the target audience for the book should be. Do I write to my Christian community or to the public at large, especially the medical and secular audience? But since this book is about sharing my experience of cancer pains, treatment, the uncertainty, my faith, and triumph during those dark days in the hospital,

I decided that the message I want to share will have a universal appeal without losing the focus on God and how He **completely** healed me of the dreaded disease, not once, but twice! (note that I used the word "completely"). I decided that there is no bigger miracle than that, and I would deny the power of God in my healing if I do not share it all. As you would see in this book, I could have died despite the care and attention I was receiving. I will share few instances when God kept me alive despite death staring me in the face and even when I lost all hope. I pray the book appeal to people of all beliefs, especially as it relates to triumph over Acute Myeloid Leukaemia. Praise God.

Joan Hunter wrote in Promises for Healing devotional that *"we live in a world that is marred by sin, which means that our bodies eventually wear out and we will eventually face death"*. It goes further to say *"Death will come to all of us, but prior to death we experience weaknesses in our physical bodies, the decay that is continually working in us. Whether cancer or a cold, diabetes, or a bone break, we all face some sort of sickness in our physical bodies"*. During my many months of stay in the hospital, it was painful for me to watch and see how my physical appearance was shrinking gradually. My bones were decaying so fast I almost started to believe what Joan said above, whether it was death knocking on my door as my body was decaying away. But glory to God this was meant to be a test of my faith and I was destined for victory.

According to Cancer Research UK, there are about two hundred different types of cancer that afflict the human body across the globe. Everywhere I have been since leaving hospital after overcoming the relapse, I have heard people marvel at my healing and the way I survived AML cancer twice. I have been told by some doctors when I visited Nigeria, that they have never seen anyone that survived leukaemia once, never mind twice. Thank God that the story ended in praise, showcasing the goodness of God upon my life. I have always been excited to share my story with everyone, and especially patients undergoing treatment for cancer. I had to develop a positive attitude towards my healing; growing my faith by focusing on the promises of God; opening and valuing the importance of family and friends support even in times of difficulty. Through the experience, I have formed an attitude of health is wealth. All these attributes are evident in this book, and I pray it blesses you as you read. I have been privileged to enjoy God's grace as in Ex 15:26 *"God promises to keep His people from diseases if we obey Him"*. Despite my shortcomings, like most people, God has been faithful to me and that is why I consider myself "a living testimony".

CHAPTER 1
BEFORE THE UPHEAVALS

"Life's trauma may seem like bitter pills to swallow. Yet God causes all things to work for our good. Our difficulties become the strong medicine for healing and spiritual growth."

Dr Millicent Hunter, bestselling author in *'Strong Medicine: Prescriptions for Successful Living'*

I would not have agreed with Dr Hunter when in September 2005 I was diagnosed with *Acute Myeloid Leukaemia* (AML) at Chase Farm Hospital in England. I felt my life journey had ended because until that point, I had only ever stayed in hospital for a few days to receive treatment for malaria and typhoid. The most recent prior to the diagnosis was a brief hospital stay in August of that year, when I was treated for malaria in Abuja, Nigeria. Unknown to me at the time I had Acute Myeloid Leukaemia.

I had a very 'interesting' upbringing. My mother was taken seriously ill when I was in modern school, and I had to leave the town of my birth for the then

Nigeria capital city of Lagos at a tender age of thirteen. Modern school was 'junior secondary school' level which most aspiring teachers attained before going to Teachers College. My three siblings and I were born into a polygamous family, my father had two wives. Poligamy in Nigeria was not strange in the rural farming community. Gaining secondary education was almost impossible despite being an 'A' grade student, because of the absence of parental guidance and support. My father, being a farmer, believed every male child he had should follow in his footsteps into farming. My mother's illness went on for most part of my growing-up years, and this was for seventeen (17) years. I mentioned these facts as a backdrop to some superstitious views expressed by family and friends when I was first diagnosed with AML. Such beliefs were inherent in Nigerian culture. I come from a rural part of Ekiti State in the South West of Nigeria, an area with a rich Yoruba culture and beliefs of mystical powers, so much so that no one dies within the community from 'natural causes. There was the belief that if someone is sick or experiencing a misfortune of any kind, it is the "supernatural" powers held by individuals in the immediate family or extended family that is responsible for that person's misfortune. Christian folks within the community will always quote the Bible and tell you that *"we fight not against flesh and blood but against principalities and powers…"*. However, the superstitious myth surrounding the Yoruba culture can take things to the extreme, not allowing for proper medical investigation and diagnosis of ailments.

My journey in the battle with cancer started way back before I was first diagnosed in September 2005. Around mid-2005, I was in Abuja on a business trip and I was staying at the home of our family friend. I woke up on the third day of my visit with remarkably high temperature; I felt dizzy and was shaking horribly. My friend had a sprawling estate, and I was staying at the guest's lodge which was far from the main house. I was in so much discomfort that I forgot my mobile phone was beside me and I did not feel strong enough to get up to use the internal telephone system to call for help. Looking back, I would have been in so much pain that affected my thinking process. I did not consider using the mobile phone that was closer to me to seek for help rather my focus was on the internal telephone system hung on the wall a few feet away from me! The first thought on my mind was that it was malaria. I was in so much pain and I had this awful thought that I could easily pass out if I did not get help quickly. At that moment, my wife called on my mobile phone and I suddenly realised that my mobile phone had been so close to me all the while. Immediately, I picked up the mobile phone and as I started speaking, my wife knew I was in trouble. She hung up the phone and called our friends at the main villa, who came round to the guest house and I was taken to a nearby hospital.

I must emphasise that many people die needlessly from curable diseases in Nigeria due to grossly inadequate health provision. Although, I was not conversant with the hospitals in Abuja, I knew that most hospitals were staffed with qualified doctors but with inadequate equipment to carry out their work. Back then, the hospitals were lacking in adequate medical facilities and infrastructure, which leads to low morale amongst health workers. In most cases, medical professionals are quick to conclude on a malaria diagnosis without carrying out tests to establish the cause of the ailment. Over the past few years however, private health provider hospitals have grown tremedously, leading to improved testing and diagnosis of cancer, and improvement in quality health services and delivery.

We go through life every day not taking stock of our physical wellbeing and ensuring that we have a healthy work-life balance. My life had always been a 'get-up-and-go' kind of hustle and I have had to fight literally for everything as there was no provision made by my parents for my education and wellbeing. I have gone through life in a tough way. So, I was resigned to the hard graft of life. I had good eyesight, never been seriously sick in my life to warrant a hospital stay, not even for one day, hence I believed I was immune from most kinds of diseases. I grew up believing any ailments could be cured with native herbal leaves called '*Agbo*', mixed with '*Ogogoro*' a local gin in Nigeria. I was born and grew up in a farming environment in a tropical landscape, so I was not afraid of any animals, including dangerous reptiles. Having survived many bruises and cuts on the farm, I thought I had grown thick skin. I thought I had an immune system that was beyond penetration by any disease. As I grew up, I had the zeal to succeed, with an ambition to become an Aeronautical Engineer. To achieve this, I literally had to learn to fend for myself from 13 years old when I left the village for Lagos. I had to work and train myself to attain secondary education. Little did I know then that I had not even begun the journey of life; little did I know that I was born (like everyone else) with cancer cells in my system which may or may never be triggered to full blown cancer, only that mine was triggered not once, but twice in ten years.

Following the health scare in Abuja, I returned to the United Kingdom, and visited my General Practitioner (GP) who carried out initial tests and asked me to return at an appointed date for the result. But before I could return to the hospital for that appointment, I fell seriously ill and I had to be taken to hospital. This was the beginning of my journey to being hospitalised at Barnet Hospital, North London, in September 2005. I spent eight months in hospital going through several courses of intense chemotherapy. I was discharged in May 2006. I was in remission for seven years until I was finally discharged in October 2013 to being fully cured from the disease. In April 2015, I was diagnosed with Secondary Relapse Acute Myeloid Leukaemia. I had to start intensive chemotherapy treatment immediately at the University College London Hospital. The rest is history, and it is a painful, life-changing experience which I will not wish for my worst enemy. I sincerely hope that sharing my experience will give hope to many who read this book, especially those suffering from similar diseases. I believe the experiences I am going to share with readers in this book will show that it is not necessarily a death sentence when there is a diagnosis for cancer. I found that in the ten years between the two cancer experiences, organisations like Cancer Research UK, Macmillan Cancer Centre and the National Health Service have undertaken ground-breaking research to improve treatment of different types of cancer. The book will encourage anyone going through difficulties that it is not over until God says it is over. I am a living testimony of God's goodness, grace, and mercy. God bless you as you read this book.

CHAPTER 2
'ONLY WHITE PEOPLE HAVE CANCER'

"I called on the Lord in my distress; the Lord answered me and set me in a broad place". Psalm 118: 5

If, like me, who sometimes ask so many questions of God, your reactions to being told you have cancer will probably be the same as mine. The sufferings of Job[1] in the Holy Bible have much to say about our natural reactions to trials and adversities of our own lives and how easy it is for us to allow them to affect our relationship with God.

---

[1] We all know the suffering of Job, his fall from grace to grass, lost all his children, wealth, and dignity, but he was resolute in standing by God even when he did not have to. He believed in God. Satan presents himself, with the sons of God, telling God that Job only fear God because he had everything all sorted out. God is truly omnipotent, trusted Job enough to ask Satan to take away everything Job had, still Job was resolute in his fear of God. In the same way, God allows sicknesses and other things to happen to us, but we must be resolute in trusting Him absolutely, so we can come out victorious as Job did.

I have always heard about people being diagnosed with various forms of life-threatening illnesses and their reaction to sudden news that will lead to a drastic change to their lifestyle. I have always wondered what it feels like and how one feels when a life-threatening diagnosis is given by doctors. Even though I know about various types of life-threatening illnesses, such as Diabetes, HIV and Acquired Immune Deficiency Syndrome (AIDS), or Sickle Cell Anaemia, nothing prepared me for receiving such devastating news! I had mixed emotions, on one hand I was told the reasons I had painful and uncomfortable symptoms over the past months; and then I am being told that I may have just weeks, months or just a few years to live. Absolutely nothing prepares one for such reality that life may end now. It was a strange feeling.

There is a history of longevity in my family because both my grandmothers died way beyond ninety-five years. My paternal grandfather died on the day I took my first walking steps in life and I understand he was in his late nineties. My maternal grandfather was my role model in the early years of my development. He would always gather us the little grandchildren together in his living room back in the village and told us stories about our cultural heritage and how much we must always believe in ourselves. He too, died at the ripe old age of ninety-three years when I was about five years old. I literarily took the family's history of longevity for granted. I was in Abuja, Nigeria when I received the news of my father's passing. I received the news of his death with great surprise as he was not incredibly old, and I was not aware he was ill. He was a farmer; a strong and healthy man and I do not remember him ever going into hospital for any treatment. I was told he died on the way to the farm. The death was sudden and there was no medical explanation given as to the cause of death, which led to speculation that 'evil people' had a hand in his death. It is important for me to point out here that because of the sudden passing of my father, I was required by tradition, to leave everything I was doing and get down to the village to attend urgent burial arrangements. I am my father's second son and his third child, so I had a particularly important role to play in making sure he was honourably buried. A bit about my father and me. It was one of those typical father-son relationships in a polygamous African setting. One of eleven children for my father and the second of four for my mother, I was a brilliant child from my early days, but my father did not know the value of education, hence there was no desire on his part to educate any of his children. He was a farmer, and his only desire was for us to continue farming with him. This led to a very frosty relationship between us. Coupled with my parents' separation and my mother's ill health, the terse relationship led to my leaving home at a young age to fend for and educate myself. Not only that, but it was also my responsibility as the eldest male child of my mother to ensure that my siblings too are looked after, ensuring their education and general wellbeing.

I left Abuja for my home state of Ekiti and myself and my siblings made necessary funeral arrangements and, my father were laid down in his final resting place, with all necessary traditional burial arrangements completed. In August, back home in England, I was having bruises all over my body, headaches, aches and pains, high temperatures and joint pains. I never really understood anything about "CANCER" because I, like most other "ignorant" people from my background, have always thought "CANCER" *was a white-only disease*! In a short period, I was spending more time at General Practitioners' (GP) surgeries and hospitals than I have ever spent all my entire life. I was in my late 40s and up to this time, I have never had or suffered any major illness other than the usual headache or malaria, as it is normal in tropical Africa. During my first visit to Chase Farm Hospital in Enfield, I was admitted immediately and went through a series of tests to establish the problem. For the whole of August 2005, I was in and out of hospital, and by now the doctors have suspected it was Leukaemia, but I was not informed. In the process, the doctors decided a bone marrow biopsy procedure was necessary. Admittedly, I had never heard of this investigative procedure. It was very painful, but I went through the procedure anyway, I had no option or a say in the matter. I had no idea what this procedure proved, but doctors were concerned that I might have cancer. I recall that after the procedure, although I was feeling pain in my buttocks and was extremely uncomfortable, I drove straight to work at Greenwich, South East London.

Following the investigation, I did not call the hospital to check the results for two reasons. First, I was afraid that the doctors would force me to come back for another bone marrow biopsy, and I was still suffering from the pains of the first one. Second, I was afraid of what the results might reveal about my health and what the actual diagnosis could be. I have heard the doctors mentioned the word 'Leukaemia' as a reason for me to have the bone marrow biopsy procedure, and I had researched what it meant, and I was not ready to be told that I have cancer of the bone marrow. The hospital called and left several messages on my mobile, and I delayed responding, because of the fear of having another big needle being stuck in my buttocks! But I was suffering so much my laptop bag became my pharmacy because I had packets of paracetamol, and other painkillers inside that I take often to relieve the pain that I was almost becoming addicted to the pain killers. I remember that as each day went by and due to the suffering, I experienced from the pain, I became a silent prayer warrior! I remember confessing, banning, and casting out all spiritual demons that were sent from Africa to afflict me. I remember that on one of those days, I took solace in reading about

Hezekiah's illness and recovery in 2 Kings Chapter 20. I was reminded that God is the author of all healing benefits and medical remedies are just an act of obedience as it was in verse 7 when Prophet Isaiah said *"Take a lump of figs. So, they took it and laid it on Hezekiah's boil, and he recovered"*. The paracetamol I was taking was like the lump of figs which I believed was going to solve my problems! Then one day, I had a call on my mobile handset but from an "unknown" number. I picked it up not knowing it was the hospital. The message from the other end of the phone was chilling and scary enough *"Is that Mr David Fadipe? Yes, I responded hesitantly,* the voice at the other hand introduced the purpose of the call and told me *'You need to come to this hospital on Thursday at 10am for another bone marrow biopsy."* This was a Tuesday, and I was to report on Thursday.

Wow! What a message to receive on the telephone! Obviously, the result of my first bone marrow biopsy was inconclusive and they wanted to repeat the procedure, just to be certain. I was scared at this point considering especially that the pains and aches in my body from the first biopsy were still fresh in my mind, and I was looking forward to Thursday's appointment with fear and trepidation. On that same day that I received the telephone call, no sooner had I got back from work that I started feeling feverish again, my temperature went through the roof, and with massive aches all over my body. My wife immediately took me to the hospital because according to her, it was as though a fire was lit beside her on the bed and it was impossible for anyone to sleep by my side on the same bed as my temperature was extremely high. On arrival at the hospital, I was admitted immediately, and I was told by the medical team that they could not understand how I was still alive with that level of temperature. I was afraid, not knowing what was coming next, but then, Psalm 73:23 came to my mind '*Yet I am always with you, you hold me by my right hand* [2]. 'The nurses took off my clothes, except my underwear and set three big fans on me, even though I was freezing inside. A series of tests were carried out at this stage and I was anxiously waiting to be told I would be okay, and that I could go home. So many Bible verses were coming to my head, but I could not speak them out.

It was later that I was told that I have cancer, and they have confirmed this by seeking a second opinion from the Royal Free Hospital in Central London. After the confirmation of the diagnosis, they said I was to be transferred to Barnet General Hospital to start my treatment and I was to be in the emergency ward until a bed could be found for me at Barnet General Hospital. That day at the emergency ward, there were weird happenings, I was put in a bed between those of two elderly people. About an hour in my waiting to be transferred, the patient on my

---

[2] Psalm 73:23 (NIV)

left died, and they cleared the bed and the area. Not long after that, the second patient on my right also passed on. I had never witnessed people dying until that day; it was very scary. It left a big impression on my mind as I witnessed the family members who had gathered to be with the person who died, leaving the room one by one and only the dead person was left with the medical staff!

I was relieved when at about 11pm they took me to Barnet with my wife driving alone behind the ambulance in the dark during gusty windy weather. This was the beginning of my treatment at Barnet General Hospital. I had no idea what the end of this journey was going to be like. Am I on my last journey? Where are they taking me to an ambulance? Is this the end? Was I going to die?

CHAPTER 3
WHY ME?

"You are my refuge and my shield; I have put my hope in your word." Ps 119:114.

Not knowing what was next, I remember this verse of the Bible and I was reciting it as I was being taken in the ambulance from Chase Farm Hospital to Barnet General Hospital. It was a very windy and wet evening. My wife was driving her car behind the ambulance through Hadley Woods to Barnet. The trees were rumbling violently because of the wind; I did not know at the time the emotional trauma my wife was going through, driving in that horrible weather alone and not knowing what would happen to me! After a difficult drive through the woods in bad weather, the ambulance parked. I had no idea where we were because, even though I worked in the London Borough of Barnet for six years in the past, I had never been to the hospital until that night!

I was admitted into the Haematology Ward at Barnet General Hospital in North London on September 16, 2005. This was the beginning of nine month stay in a strange environment considering I have never spent over one week in the hospital prior to this day! On the diagnosis, doctors told me I had a thirty percent chance of surviving. Remember the thirty percent, that was the slimmest chance I was given to live. Technically, I was already seventy percent closer to death than life. On the night I was admitted, the doctors spent the first few hours of my admission explaining my treatment plan over the next few months. They did not know how long the treatment was going to take, this was dependant on how I respond to the treatment. I was told that I would go through four cycles of chemotherapy administration, and that I might also be asked to take part in the ongoing trial of new drugs as treatment proceeds. The doctors to me that it was normal practice for patient to have full briefing of treatment process and details on diagnosis of a major illness like mine, What I was not prepared for, was the entourage of medical personnel that came to give me that briefing! The consultant was followed by a retinue of two other doctors, about three Nurses, a counselling staff, and a psychiatrist! I was panicky on seeing this large number of medical personnel come to my room just to brief me about the treatment. It was a good thing that the Doctor noticed my fear and explained to me that this briefing was necessary, as part of their professional obligations to me as patient, but at that time, it was all new to me. And because this was a new territory for me, it was scarier to listen to the pre-treatment briefing by these groups of people who have descended on my room. Pre-treatment briefing was to cover areas of the type of chemotherapy drugs that will be administered and the method in which it would be administered over the period of stay in the hospital. Chemotherapy is usually given through a drip into a vein in the arm, or sometimes into a major vein via a semi-permanent central line such as Hickman line or Porta Cath, depending on the complexity of the illness. Mine was the latter case where I had to have the Hickman line installed in my vein. The most traumatic part of the pre-treatment briefing was the explanations of the most common side effects of chemotherapy administration, to the point where it was safe to ask if there was any point in going through this treatment at all. If this treatment was meant to kill and destroy cancer cells, why does the same drug cause so many adverse side effects?

Ironically, some of the side effects of the pre-treatment briefing gave me the chills! The enormity of the stark realities of the adverse side effects I was about to face.

- Feeling sick – Nausea and vomiting: The doctors assured that not all chemotherapy drugs will make one feel sick or be sick, but there was possibility of that in this case because of the type of chemotherapy drug I was on at the time, but there was the relief of anti-sickness drugs to prevent the problem

- Possible temporary or permanent loss of hair. This was not funny as I could not imagine at the time that there was going to be a time my fine afro hair would disappear. Growing up you see older people who had no hair and used to be childishly cynical about it. To now think that this illness will cause me to lose all hair was unthinkable but also unavoidable, but I prayed for complete healing from hair loss and I think God answered!
- Tiredness was said to be one of the most common side effects of chemotherapy. But I thought that being tired and feeling sorry for myself was never going to be an option.
- Fertility or Infertility. This was probably more difficult to accept at the time as my wife and I were still looking to God for His blessings in this department. It was said that chemotherapy often makes the patient temporarily infertile and can be permanent in some cases. This was scary but according to the advice of the doctors, we were given the opportunity for sperm storage pre-treatment for future use. In all things the name of God is glorified
- There were other adverse effects such as Strange taste changes in the mouth; Sore mouth; Loss of Appetite; Altered Bowel habit; Phlebitis (sore veins) and so on. All I could remember was this awful feeling of fear, trepidation and despair running through my head, while trying to make sense of what I have just been told. I

pondered; will I survive this illness? Was this the end? I am in my late forties, I have not achieved all my aspirations in life, it was not my time because I was nowhere near ready to die!

The information I was given aroused a lot of frustration and anger in me, and I queried God endlessly. For one entire week of my admission, I kept asking God questions like, why me? What did I do wrong to deserve this? Haven't I seen enough trials and tribulations in my life, after everything I had been through from my youthful years? My wife too was worried because of the uncertainty of the outcome of the treatment. She too did not know what was happening and how things were going to pan out. I refused to eat because I was angry, and I could not be bothered by what happened to me. I had given up. I asked these questions but was getting no answers, until the middle of the night on my 7th day of admission! I had barely closed my eyes when a clear voice came to me, "*you keep asking why me, why me? Why not you? Don't you think this is happening to you so that God can glorify Himself?*" and I believe this to be God speaking to me.

Wow! I opened my eyes and realised I had just had an encounter with God. In the middle of my frustration and anger, I was having a conversation with God. I recalled Psalm 118:5 which states, '*I called on the Lord in distress; The Lord answered me and set me in a broad place.*". It was like my eyes have just been opened to the glory of the Lord, that where I gave up was where He was starting. I read the same Psalm 118 again and came across verses 17 and 18: "*I shall not die, but live. And declare the works of the Lord. The Lord has chastened me severely, but He has not given me over to death*". The next morning, my wife came visiting, and she told me that as she was falling asleep, she heard these words "*it is not unto death*" she was startled and decided to read the bible to get back to sleep. As she read Isaiah 30:15 the following words stuck in her mind '*In quietness and confidence shall be your strength*'. She told me she meditated on the word and she drew great fortitude from it, because it reminded her that our confidence should be in God's ability to heal me. This gave us strength. The Lord speaks to our situation all the time, but we need to be attentive to the tune of the Holy Spirit. It was at this point I asked God to forgive me for complaining. I asked Him to heal me according to His words. Mind you, I was still afraid and unsure of what the future holds especially with the prognosis, but I was now less worried about this dreaded disease, rather I was now focussed on accepting the situation and focusing on the treatment plans that have been put together for me by my doctors.

1. I spent the following days and weeks studying the word of God, and being more positive about my treatment, taking in all God's promises for

my healing through His words. The numerous side effects of chemotherapy told me during that pre-treatment briefing kept ringing in my head, but It got better with the application of God's words. Thirty percent chance of surviving the disease at diagnosis, and even if I survive, there were other possible adverse effects that could affect me for the rest of my life.

2. Possible loss of hair, or suffer from severe hair loss which may never grow my hair again
3. Chances of never been able to produce enough strong sperm to father a child ever again! This was difficult to take as I was still hoping for us to try again and again for that precious gift of child from the Lord.

The following day, I was taken in an ambulance to the Reproductive Clinic at the University College London Hospital, where I gave sperm samples for storage for future artificial insemination in case my wife needs to take that option if I do not make it through this disease. That was the first-time visiting University College London Hospital, even though I had lived in the United Kingdom all my adult life. University College London Hospital would later become my second home ten years later; more on that later in this book.

On returning to Barnet General Hospital, I had a minor operation to fix what was called the "Hickman

Line". This was a form of canular for the administration of chemotherapy into my blood system. Chemotherapy can only be administered through the canular system and not by mouth or any naked administration into the body. This is because it is poisonous and it kills all cells in the body, including cancer cells and other living cells. The next day, my treatment started. I was in a strange environment, now the decision is out of my hands, there was nothing I could do, other than to obey and listen to the doctors who were taking care of me, and above all, read God's word and discern what He is saying to me through the words. Let me tell you, this was the first time I dwelt in God's words so much and read the whole of Psalm 119 several times. I was determined that if I was going to die, I was going to know God's words, bury my hope in His words till the end, so that when I get into heaven, I will be able to join the saints and sing Glory, Glory, Lord God Almighty! Following admission at Barnet general Hospital, I called our pastor at the Kings House, Edmonton, Pastor Tony Peters, who came and spent time praying with me and anointed me with oil.

One thing I had so much on my hands at this time was TIME, which I tried hard as I can, to invest on God's words, I was also experiencing some revelations about "Sickness", the family of which this Cancer bedevilling me comes from. I understood that *we live in a world that is marred by sin, so our bodies wear out and we will eventually face death*.

But prior to death we experience weakness in our physical bodies, the decay that is continually working in us. It could be Blood Cancer (like mine), or a cold, diabetes and even just a fracture, but we all face sickness in our physical bodies. But I took hold of God words in Hebrews 4:16 that says: *"Let us approach the throne of grace with confidence, so we may receive and find grace to help us in our time of need"*. This is my time of need, more than ever. Need for revelation of God's word, need to find God truly, need to hear from God about my condition, and above all, need to be healed! I submitted myself to the painful experience of cancer treatment through chemotherapy, not that I have any other option. The first few weeks were particularly challenging. I experienced pain as I have never experienced it before, I lost my lovely Afro black hair in less than a month, I looked in the mirror and did not recognise the person I was looking at staring at me in the mirror, and what a charcoal dark skeleton I had become!

Let us face it, cancer is evil. I have been transformed into an unfamiliar creature and I could see that the usually robust me was gone; I had almost turned into a skeleton. I realise why people die once they have been diagnosed with any form of cancer. I realise it is not the actual disease that kills so fast but the fear of it. It was a harrowing experience and one that cannot be wished for my worst enemy if ever there was one! I was in a room by myself as I could not be in an open ward because of the risk of infection.

There were other patients suffering different types of cancer like mine who were also in the adjoining private rooms at the Haematology Ward at Barnet General Hospital. It amazed me that out of all the patients having treatment at that time, I was one of just three who survived and got discharged after the treatment, Praise God. This is not to belittle the grace of God on my life, truly I do not understand why God loves me so much and spared my life. But also, there came a realisation that sickness makes us closer to God! I had read the Bible from Genesis to Revelation at least once prior to my illness. I read it as a matter of necessity, not to allow God to minister to me through His word. It was an accepted practice of a new believer to read the Bible in one year. Well, that was me. Only that this time, I was reading with the weight of my affliction upon me, and sincerely seeking God to reveal to me His plan and purpose. I kept proclaiming from Isaiah 53:5, "by his stripes *I am healed*[3] ", whilst at the same time asking God that if these words were true, why am I in this position now? It was difficult to trust and believe but I also knew there was no option other than for me to trust God and his words. I did not have to understand what was happening to me or why it was happening. I knew I had to trust God despite what is happening to me; not because of what He has done or had not done, but because of who He is, Lord over all. I had

---

[3] Isaiah 53 v5 - But He was pierced for our transgression, He was crushed for our iniquities, the punishment that brought us peace was on Him, and by His wounds we are healed

to call on God[4] and claim the promises of God for my healing through his words[5] I wanted to be healed so desperately just so I could proclaim God's glory. It is amazing how much of a prayer warrior we become when faced with difficult situations, especially life-threatening ones. We need to understand that we are more focussed on God when we think life is leaving us and it is not meant to be like that. Charles Capps (1991)[6] wrote in his book that God's word is creative power. The world was framed and formed by the word of God. Confessing the word of God can also change our world even as it changed my hopelessness to victory over cancer. It changed the image of sickness in my mind into an image of healing and health. But why do we wait until we are in difficulties before we take this word of God seriously for our healing medicine? Sure, it is difficult to operate on these principles, it takes discipline and commitment. Charles Capps maintained it is not good enough to just read these confessions of the word, he encouraged us to confess the **word** audibly and with authority.

I understand that in any situation we found ourselves, our faith in God and the belief that He cares for us

---

[4] Let us therefore come boldly to the throne of grace, that we may obtain mercy and find grace to help in time of need" Hebrews 4: 16

[5] It is the Spirit who gives life; the flesh profits nothing. The words that I speak to you are spirit, and they are life" John 6: 63

[6] God's Creative Power for Healing; Charles Capps 1991 published by Harrison House Inc

will normally see us through. It is important to form an ***attitude of positive confessions*** as a daily routine because I learnt from my experience of cancer that it is all about a positive attitude and positive confession. My faith became stronger as I went through the treatment, and I believe this mindset and faith has been with me since, helping me to go through the secondary relapsed cancer ten years later, which I will elaborate on in the latter part of this book.

"Oh, gives thanks to the Lord, for He is good! For His mercy endures forever" (Ps 118: 29)

The early days of being in hospital went by in a haze. Eight weeks into my first treatment of cancer, after finishing the first of four courses of aggressive chemotherapy which had killed some cancerous and other living cells in my body; I was completely Neutropenic.[7] and weak. I had no energy left; I was fragile, but I was told that I was on a journey of recovery to growing back some new cells for energy. It was a painful waiting experience, and it gave me even more time to focus on God. It was normal practice to allow some days off from the hospital and to go home after completing each circle of the chemotherapy treatment; so, I was allowed home for

---

[7] Neutropenia is an abnormally low concentration of neutrophils (a type of white blood cell) in the blood. Neutrophils make up the majority of circulating white blood cells and serve as the primary defence against infections by destroying bacteria, bacterial fragments, and immunoglobulin-bound viruses in the blood - *Wikipedia*).

ten days after spending about eight weeks in the hospital. It was during my stay at home that I wrote a testimony for my church magazine. It is important to always trust God because this period was just the beginning, and I had no idea what the rest of the treatment was going to bring. I knew I was given a thirty percent chance of surviving this disease when I was diagnosed, and that has changed little even after the first cycle of chemotherapy. But I was confident in God's promises enough to put my testimony into writing, and which was published in the King's House, Edmonton Church newsletter of December 2005.

CHAPTER 4
STEADFAST IN FAITH

"Be sober, be vigilant; because your adversary the devil walks about like a roaring lion, seeking whom to devour. 1 Peter 5: 8

I have never fully understood why God allowed Job to go through all that suffering until I read in Dr Hunter's book that *"It was Satan trying to convince Job through his sufferings that God's governing of the world was unjust."* Incidentally, my experiences whilst lying down on the hospital bed has been that things happen to us sometimes, God allows things to happen so we can be reconciled with God the father, so that like Job, God's character can be developed in us through the adversities that we go through. My experiences going through the pains and treatment of cancer taught me that 'For *all the promises of God in Him are Yes, and in Him Amen, to the glory of God through us* (2 Cor 1:20). Many of us do not prepare for trauma or sickness because we do not realise that trials can come because of satanic attacks. Whereas the Bible warns us to be vigilant and watch out for his schemes. *"Resist him, steadfast in the faith, knowing that the same sufferings are experienced by your brotherhood in the world*" (1 Peter 5:9 NKJV)[8]. This verse became my cornerstone whilst in hospital and you shall know why as you read this book.

Sometimes also, we physically punish our body and take little or no care of it at all. We forget that our body also experiences wear and tear, due for repair or MOT! Yes, our body is the temple of God, but we must look after this temple always, both spiritually and physically. It is important to go for medical check-ups of our body regularly just as we do our cars. You may be spirit-filled, Bible-believing, tongue-speaking born-again Christian, but you are not immune to sickness; sickness will attack your physical body unless you are vigilant as Peter said in 1 Pet 5: 8 above. We must always involve ourselves in light forms of physical exercise to relieve the stress of everyday life. I endeavour to go for walks regularly and purposefully undertake domestic chores that are rigorous. I intend to do more physical exercise as I consider I can do more to be healthy. I hope as you read this book, you will find more ways to increase physical exercise. Now let us look at how God dealt with my mindset, my spirit and my whole being whilst in hospital. It was daunting for me to understand why this should happen to me; I remember JESUS walking on water after He told His disciples to go ahead of him in *Matt 14: 22-31.*

---

[8] 1 Peter 5:9

But like Peter and the rest of the disciples, I doubted for a minute, until I heard God said to me *"O you of little faith, why did you doubt?" Verse 31.* Then I decided I was going into the next treatment cycle focussing on the other side rather than the raging sea ahead (chemotherapy treatment), which I believe *JESUS* has calmed down for my sake.

During my subsequent treatment cycles, I had various encounters with God. This was truly a time of reckoning for me and it coincided with the time of aggressive chemotherapy treatment. This period, according to the experts, is what determines how well the patient will respond to the treatment. I thank Almighty God for my family who were around me. To have people close to me whom I can relate and talk to, helped me on my journey. Believe me, this was a journey I did not know the destination, except my hope and expectations of the outcome I wanted at the end of the journey. My family, friends and church members were my regular source of strength and support during that difficult and energy-sapping hospital stay. The nurses were fantastic, I do not know how they do their jobs but those in the nursing profession are the most caring people I know. The first few weeks were with mixed feelings and I must admit I did not know what to expect. I prayed, I believed, and I read the Word, yet I still did not know what to expect! I spent time personalising and meditating on *Romans 8: 37 "Yet in all these things we are more than conquerors through Him who loved us"*. Although I was told constantly that it was early days, I started to lose a bit of hair and my appetite.

One day, as I was watching a programme called *City Hospital* on daytime TV (normally I hardly watch daytime TV), but this is an uncommon situation, a different era. Time has changed, and now that I was stuck in the hospital, watching daytime TV has become my pastime. Anyway, on the TV screen was a 34-year-old mixed-race man going through similar treatment for Acute Myeloid Leukaemia. He was desperate for a stem cell donor as the 'experts' told him his survival depended on finding a donor! What news to hear on national television at a critical point of my treatment. This brings me to another important point; like me, most black people do not donate blood, do not donate bone marrows, do not donate eggs or embryos or kidneys. Donating could make a difference to someone's life whether he lives or dies, and all that is required is some cases is disruption to our daily routine.

Anyway, back to the man on television. Whilst the programme was ongoing, he was appealing for a donor to come to his aid. I felt sad and upset, considering that I was going through the same illness. Then I turned off the TV and got hold of my Spirit-Filled Bible, flipped open and Wow! on the very first page I turned to, were these *words "I shall not die, but live, and declare the Glory of the Lord"*

Ps 118:17. (some translations say, "And declare the **Works** *of the Lord").* I knew the words were for me, to comfort and reassure me and I claimed it straight away. And my distress went away faster than it came.

Towards the end of that week, I was full of thanksgiving in faith and belief that God has healed me. I remember reading the story of King David dancing in his courtyard because of the return of the Ark of the Covenant in 2 Samuel 6: 16 – 19; and David sure knows how to praise God. At this time, I just felt like breakdancing! Praise is the answer to relieve a weakened and tired body like mine after having gone through the first and second cycles of intensive treatment. I remember waking up one morning with Jeremiah's prayer of deliverance, *"Heal me O Lord, and I shall be healed. Save me and I shall be saved; for You are my praise"* (Jeremiah 17:14). *Surely, the Lord is close to those who trust in Him. I put my trust in You that I will not go through all the horrible side effects that the Doctors have predicted*! I rested all week because my cells were destroyed by the aggressive dose of chemotherapy and I had become completely neutropenic. My immune system was non-existent, and I later learnt that this period was one of the most dangerous stages of the treatment because of the risk of infection. Every single one of my visitors had to wear protective clothing and gloves so that they do not transfer infection to me. The doctors were amazed that the side effects I had were minor and not significant. Praise God!

The periods after each cycle of chemotherapy were always very tiring for there is not much to do. I usually spend the time to read the bible, newspapers, books, sleep, think, watch daytime television (again and again), and watched music videos and some Nollywood movies. But it is good to dwell in the word of God because it was more of my antibiotic than those given by doctors. God moved in His Glory and Power in the hospital because He made me a breath of fresh air to the Nurses and Doctors! I sold Christian music video from my hospital bed and lives were touched around me in that period. I had to request more copies from the bookshop we owned at that time to meet the request. I thank God for using me as a vessel to achieve His purpose even while in a hospital bed. I started making notes of daily events in the hospital after the first two cycles of chemotherapy, experiences which have now come together in this book. Honestly, I was not aware of the challenges still ahead before the illness called leukaemia was finally defeated in my life. This is more of a testimony to encourage brethren that wherever we are, God is there with us when we call upon Him. I like what Charles Capps wrote in his book, *'God's creative power for healing'*. On Page 12, he had written *"God did not send His word to heal but he sent His word and Healed. God considers it done"*. My healing resulted from several things, my attitude, my faith, and to a large extent, my faith in the expertise of the doctors and nurses who treated me through the National Health Service (NHS England).

CHAPTER 5
ENDURANCE TEST

"And the peace of God which transcends all understanding, will guard your hearts and mind in Christ Jesus." Phil 4: 7

Medical science aids healing through physical means of administering medicine into the physical body[9]. I have now completed the first two cycles of the four-cycle treatment and I was discharged to go home for the usual ten-day recuperation time called respite period! I was pleased that the time to be spent at home coincided with the Christmas holiday season, because I was already dreading the thought of spending Christmas and New Year holidays in the hospital room, which could be very lonely. Weekends in hospitals are the most boring, lonesome, and sometimes worrying period for a patient, especially those on life-threatening illness. The hospital ward is usually not as busy over the weekend as the case was on weekdays, although I never really thought about it at the time. When I thought I would spend

---

[9] Charles Capps p12.

Christmas on the hospital bed, I allowed God's peace which transcends all understanding to guard my heart and mind.[10] Praise God! I ended up spending two weeks at home. Feeling frail, I knew I had lost the 'Me' that I was before hospital admission. I looked in the mirror and could not recognise the person staring back at me in the mirror. It was a very traumatic experience, but I had to put on a brave face, and that was every time we had visitors come around. We had several well-wishers who came to visit, fellowship, and prayed with us.

Before the end of the second chemotherapy treatment cycle, the doctors sat me down and told me they were considering putting me on trial for a new drug for the third treatment cycle. The drug was a new American drug called ARA C. They were considering putting me on the trial because they thought they needed to be more aggressive with the treatment, as my siblings could not provide a 100 percent match for stem cell transplant the doctors concluded that the new drug was worth a try to improve my chances of surviving the cancer. I had conflicting emotions about the new drug, especially considering the pain that I had gone through with tried and tested drugs in my last two treatment cycles. So, the question on my mind was whether this new drug will be more painful or whether it will bring relief to my pains. I concluded that there was nothing to lose with my involvement

---

[10] Phil 4: 7

in the trial drug because it was worth the risk I thought, consoling myself by remembering Jesus has borne all our sickness, and our sins[11].

Throughout my ten days' stay at home, I was preoccupied with the thought of the new drug trial I would be involved in when I got back into hospital. I went into hospital as early as possible, to get full information and counselling from doctors about the risks and rewards of the new drug trial. There was limited information on what this new drug will achieve other than what the drug is called, and it comes from the United States of America. That was about the best information I had at my disposal. I had full counselling and information about the new trial drug which was called ARA C. The trial drug has just been released after extensive research at the American Society for Cancer Research. It was a more powerful drug than the previous chemotherapy drug I had in the two previous treatment cycles. Now it is important to remember that God heals by many means, either by answering our prayer of faith with miraculous healing; natural recuperative powers which I had to develop from within me with my attitude and resilience; and medical aid which I am getting from the doctors and nurses who are the experts in that area. Whilst I was not sure of the outcome of the new drug, I had to cultivate a *positive attitude* towards the outcome of

---

[11] Mathew 8: 17b says that "He took up our infirmities and bore our diseases".

the drug for my healing. The treatment of the new trial drug has started. I had so many experiences during treatment with the drug which are worth mentioning. Of importance was that I experienced a lot of difficulties, pain and miracles all rolled into one during this period. Let me provide a little more detail on the experiences that I had during this third cycle of chemotherapy.

PAIN TO PRAISE

"If the music is the food of love, then play on." (The first line of the play Twelfth Night, by William Shakespeare)

I encountered God in a new way through gospel music whilst lying down on that hospital bed at Barnet General, unsure of what lay ahead of me. Listening to gospel music was very relaxing and it usually takes my mind away from the pain and discomfort of treatment. What I had on this day was a life-changing and faith-strengthening experience. Three days after I started the ARA C treatment cycle, my brother and his wife arrived from Nigeria and came to see me in hospital. They spent some time with me, and they were extremely shocked to see me looking so ill. They were in tears and I had to encourage them, despite my pain, that I was fine, and I would be okay. Really? Was I fine? Would I really be okay? But I had to believe I had to exercise faith. Anything to the contrary was counterproductive, especially remembering the revelations my wife had at the beginning of this whole trial, that it was ***not unto death***. Each time I had visitors, I tried to act normally, because I realised that I was not the only one suffering. My immediate family members were probably suffering too.

My wife and my siblings were in my hospital room on a particular evening. They were there with me till what seemed like an eternity. I wanted to be left alone so I could be on my own and be left in peace, to go through what I was going through alone. It wanted to cry my eyes out because I did not know which part of my body the pain was coming from, all I knew was that I had pains and aches all over, and I wanted my family to leave so I can just cry to sleep. So, by around 9.30 pm, I had to whisper to one of the nurses to tell them I needed a rest, so that they can leave. Before they left, my brother gave me some video that he brought from Nigeria. Thank God my wife made sure I had a television set and a Digital Versatile Disk (DVD) player in the room for my convenience. Until that day, I had listened to, and enjoyed mainly western gospel music such as Hillsongs, Don Moen and other popular gospel artists. So, I slotted one of the DVD into the DVD players. I was greeted with the best Yoruba Afro beat gospel music I have ever heard, full of encouraging and motivational messages that was so appropriate for the situation I was experiencing. I had never heard about the artist playing the music, nor his brand of music. The music was titled Fulfilment, and it was by a popular Nigerian Gospel music artist,

Yinka Ayefele! I enjoyed the music so much and wish I could just get up and dance, but my body felt too weak that I could not get up. I was transfixed while listening to the testimonial lyrics and watching people dancing so joyfully, except the lead singer himself, Yinka Ayefele whom I observed was not dancing. Out of curiosity, I called my brother on the telephone to thank him for bringing such encouraging music to me, I also asked him why the lead singer was on a wheelchair and not dancing like the others. My brother then dropped a bombshell that Yinka Ayefele was involved in an accident and he is paralysed from the waist down! Oh My God, I shouted. What? Paralysed? OMG! It was at this point I called on God that if Yinka Ayefele who was paralysed from the waist down, can sing praises on to the Lord so powerfully, who am I not to sing praises unto His name. I fell in love with Yinka Ayefele and his music from that day, and I have introduced his music to almost everyone I know. I know I will meet Mr Ayefele someday to let him know the impact his music had on my life and my healing at such an exceedingly difficult and seemingly hopeless time. *https://soundcloud.com/ rog-dee/yinka-ayefele-fulfilment-official-video*

FAMILIES SUFFER TOO

Dr Millicent Hunter wrote "sickness is a punishment of transgression; but repentance can bring healing"[12].

---

[12] Millicent Hunter

Sometimes when we go through difficulties in life, whether illness or hardship, we become very selfish and self-centred. While I was in hospital, it was all about me; I felt the entire world owed me a favour. I did not spare a thought for the pain and stress that those around me were going through. I did not realise that they were suffering just as much as I was suffering too. Obviously, they were hopeless and helpless just like I was, looking at me just like I was looking at them. Sometimes there was not much to be said, and someone will say "Let us pray". Prayer was always the easiest conversation topic that anyone can think of. Then one evening my wife came to see me on a wet and windy evening; she was late bringing me some home cooked dinner, which she brought every day, after a long day at the office, as hospital food was not palatable. I flared up and took all my frustrations out on her, but she politely apologised for coming late. I ate the food, and she left. About fifteen minutes after she left my room, I looked out of the window into the hospital car park, I did not understand why I did that because it was unusual for me to do so especially at that time of day. I saw my wife standing by her car, unable to get into the car and drive. Even from afar, I could see she was extremely exhausted and tired. I felt so guilty and I cried out for repentance to God to forgive me for being so selfish and ignorant, so much that I could not see that this woman was suffering! I could not fathom the fact that even though I was the one going through cancer treatment and everybody around me were doing their absolute best empathising with me, I could not see that deep down those close to me were suffering a different type of pain. The pain of helplessness, anxiety and to an extent, grief. Neither me nor those around me knew what was going to happen. I am sure they too were asking the same questions I asked myself daily. Would I survive this? Later, that night, I called my wife on the phone, I expressed to her that I was glad she got home safely. I confessed my sense of guilt to her and apologised for the way I had treated her all because of the pain and frustrations I was experiencing. It is important for us to understand that the pain of sickness is not limited to the sufferer, the carers suffer too.

"Rejoice in hope, be patient in tribulation, be constant in prayer" (Romans 12:12).

The third experience I had during this period was the most terrifying and the above bible verse explains it well. I was hoping that the trial drug will be much better than previous treatment cycles although I was not sure I was rejoicing in that hope. Was I patient in the tribulation that I was afflicted with? Well, I really did not have a choice because all I could do at the time was to be patient and constant in prayer. Something happened during this period that nearly led to my death. It was on a Saturday afternoon and as usual, the Haematology Ward had skeletal staff over the weekend and mobile telephones were not as sophisticated as they are today, because you may never get network to call or receive calls due to the interference of the medical equipment in the hospital ward. On that day, I was given a big dose of ARA C chemotherapy drug through the Hickman line which was fixed into my veins on top of my left breast. The administration of the drug usually takes as long as five hours. So, the nurse on duty affixed the drug on me at about 12 noon that faithful Saturday afternoon, programmed it to last for four hours. She came back to check on me, and how I was doing, and to clamp back the intravenous at the expiration of the four-hour drug administration, this was to stop any outflow of blood from my body once the full chemotherapy bag has been fully infused.

I was extremely tired and weak, and I laid down listening to music, imagining what the world would have been like with no disease if Adam and Eve have not sinned. The time I lay waiting for the chemotherapy to be administered were the longest I had ever waited for anything in my entire life. It usually feels like eternity because the pain I was experiencing was slow, though unseen. I did everything from listening to music, reflecting, reading and finally fell asleep because of my weakened body! That was about 2.30 pm, I still had about ninety minutes before the drug was fully infused into my body. I fell asleep as the drug was pumped into my body. I heard the phone ringing, and I woke up. My phone was ringing non-stop, as I reached out to the table to pick my phone to answer the call, I realised I could not move. I felt heavily laden and weak. I felt as if I was swimming inside the Atlantic Ocean because my bed was wet and all the clothes I wore, and the duvet cover were soaking wet, WITH MY BLOOD! Psalm 118: 17 says *"I shall not die but live, to declare the glory of the Lord"*. Apparently, the whole chemotherapy bag has been infused into my system and the machine had stopped dead on 4 pm, but the Nurse who came and clamped up the Hickman line forgot to come back at the appropriate time, and my blood came out through the intravenous system and started dripping on the bed, on the mattress and then onto the floor. I could not remember how I reached for the bell to call for the nurses' attention that afternoon. I was dangerously close to passing out in my own blood, but God is faithful. By the time a nurse responded to the bell, I understood that I already passed out. I understood that the nurse herself was distraught, scared and thought I was dead. Remember, I mentioned earlier that this was on a Saturday; the only doctor on call was a Registrar. I later learnt from my wife, that she felt a burden on her spirit to call me and she called and kept on calling until I answered. Praise God, that God used another incidental call to save my life.

Usually, weekends in the ward were always quieter than weekdays because patients who are stable enough tend to go home for the weekend if they are not in neutropenic stage. The nurse cleaned me up, moved me into another bed and cleaned out the room. I had to be given about six litres of water and two bags of blood immediately. The testimony behind this experience was that God continues to glorify Himself through my healing.

There were several other difficulties and challenges that I encountered during this trial drug cycle, but in all of it, God saved and delivered me. The third cycle of treatment was much longer because of the new drug trial and the difficulties I encountered. I was in hospital for eight weeks for this cycle, instead of the 6 weeks for the previous cycles. But one thing was constant in my behaviour even during that trying and uncertain period, praising God and singing gospel songs was a big relief. I was in isolation during the time because I was completely neutropenic, with no immunity at all to fight any infection. I was allowed home for a period of seven days to recuperate, to prepare for the fourth and final chemotherapy cycle of treatment.

CHAPTER 6
ATTITUDE ADJUSTMENT

"You are bought with a price: therefore, glorify God in your body, and in your spirit, which are God's". 1 Cor 6:20

I was admitted back into the hospital for the fourth and final cycle of chemotherapy treatment after resting at home for ten days, ten instead of seven because the hospital called to delay my readmission for this final chemotherapy cycle. Following a series of blood tests, including the tests carried out on my two siblings to find out if either of them could be a donor, I am now putting my hope in this last cycle of chemotherapy to get rid of the cancer cells. The doctors have concluded that only one of my siblings has a fifty percent match as a donor and this was not adequate to perform a transplant operation, all my hopes of living now rest on this last cycle of treatment. The doctors also concluded that using the trial drug for the third chemotherapy treatment cycle may be enough to destroy the remaining cancer cells, which means the need for a stem cell transplant was not needed. This represented a minor consolation and encouragement even though I was still overwhelmed with uncertainty about the future, and questioning why, why, why? I was feeling encouraged by the word of God which constantly speaks to me about the miraculous healings through faith and work of God contained in several Bible scriptures. I knew I had to have faith, I knew I had to live by faith, I knew I had to believe that *"this was Not unto Death"*. I wanted God's word to be the source of my supernatural help because I could not afford to give up. I felt there had to be a better plan of God waiting in store for me, I knew I had promise and hope, I knew I had to get past this illness, I had to survive, I had to live, I must be a **Living Testimony**. It was hard believing all the aforementioned, however I realised I had no alternative other than to develop and maintain a positive mindset.

It has been over four years since I left hospital as I write this portion of the book. Coincidentally, reading the '*Word for Today*' on my Bible App, it is about '*Attitude adjustment.*' It talks about Air Traffic Controllers seeing the bigger picture for what is going on in the sky and on ground. They have the knowledge and authority to guide pilots to slow down or speed up, fly higher or lower to avoid or navigate through storms, or to take alternative routes. With so many flights simultaneously taking up and landing every minute, pilots must stay in touch with the control tower. Similarly, I had to stay with God's word even during my period of despair on the hospital bed, because He alone could see the bigger picture of my life and orchestrate all that concerns me, including the illness that I went through. During my trials, I was like a passenger in an aeroplane who cannot do anything about falling off the sky once the plane leaves the ground, all hopes for safe landing now rest in the pilot's hand. I felt if I could trust a human being to fly an aeroplane and land it safely several hours later, then I must trust God to see me through this last huddle. Once I have conditioned my mind to have faith in God and trust him with my life, I felt stronger and was encouraged to go into my last treatment cycle. I was encouraged by God's words declared through the following verses:

1. *"Fear not, for I am with you. Be not dismayed, for I am your God. I will strengthen you, yes I will help you, I will uphold you with My righteous right hand".* Isaiah 41:10
2. *"Surely He took up our pains and bore our sufferings,"* First part of Isaiah 53:4
3. Jer. 30:17 *"I will restore you to health and heal your wounds."* Jer. 30:17

Surely, my positive attitude was not by my strength because I had none. Without God being my strength, I do not know how I would have coped. Indeed, it was *"Not by might nor by power, but by God's spirit* (Zechariah 4:6).

One particularly saddening issue at this stage was that two of the other eight patients that were admitted at the same time with me died. The Haematology Ward had been my home for the past seven months. We met in the common room when we were not neutropenic, ate together and we went through treatment and pains together. Suffice it to say that adversity brought us together, and we became friends, sharing treatment experiences together and encouraging each other. We have bonded so well, hoping to see each other again at the other side of life, with the hope of overcoming this disease. I remember we used to discuss how we would feel when the treatment was completed, and we finally get discharged to the clinic.

I was close to a young Jewish lady who had so much trouble getting through the treatment. She was in her early twenties, and it broke my heart to see such a young and petite lady in so much pain from debilitating cancer. Even though I was going through my own problems and unsure of what was going to happen, I felt that this young lady did not deserve to be going through this pain. I mean what has she done to deserve this? I wondered why a young person with no history of smoking or drinking would suffer from cancer. Again, this was part of my ignorance about this dreaded disease, I always thought cancer was caused by either smoking, or other bad habits. She had massive problems coping with the pain of her treatment. She was always down for many more days being neutropenic after each cycle of treatment, so it took her much longer to recover and grow her immunity back. It is amazing how cancer treatment or being in hospital can bring perfect strangers together and make them friends. Because we spent most of our time talking about our treatment, our pains, our doubts, our expectations, our hopes for survival and especially, we talked about the day we will finish our treatment and meet up at the Day Clinic. But then we were all in an uncertain environment, not knowing what happens next. It was normal to be having lunch with someone (a co-patient) at 1pm and then at 5pm, the same patient has had complications in treatment and has been moved to the Intensive Care Unit (ICU). Two hours later you hear the patient was dead! It was that bad. I am writing this portion of the book at the time the entire world is battling with Coronavirus Pandemic. I sometimes remember those times in hospital when Intensive Care Unit (ICU) seemed to be the gate to dying. So, when I hear on the news that someone has been taken to ICU, I worry, even though I know the love of God casts out all fears. Treatment in every area of health care has advanced and Intensive Care Unit is no longer a passage to death. Praise God!

Those situations and the deaths created a lot of anxiety and tension' It was like, who is next? Those of us who identified as Christians constantly prayed together, using God's words to console each other. *"The Lord is near to all who call on him, to all who call on Him in truth"* Psalm 145: 18 NIV. We had our hopes built on these words and it lifted us up each time anyone in the ward is down or struggling with treatment. Please remember this was the period for the last of my four chemotherapy cycles. It was already concluded that I would no longer have any stem cell transplant since there was no 100% match either from my siblings or from within the African Caribbean blood cell bank. The doctors have concluded that the four cycles of chemotherapy were enough treatment to cleanse me of the leukaemia cells. Knowledge of the above situations did not make the treatment easier; I still had anxieties, and I was expectant, but I hoped that God was going to save me. However, as each day passed, I kept hold and affirmed God's words that this was NOT UNTO DEATH, Praise God! By the beginning of April 2006, I completed the chemotherapy treatment and as usual, became completely neutropenic, lost my immunity because of the full chemotherapy, the journey to grow back my immunity cells has just begun.

By this time, growing back my cells was more difficult because for the fourth time in a matter of eight (8) months, my body has been bruised and battered by the aggressive chemotherapy treatment. I spent the following five weeks being neutropenic. It took much longer this time to recover from the last cycle of chemotherapy. I could not eat properly; I felt frail and weak, but God is my strength. I was now more optimistic that I will survive this, despite the fragile state of my being. I was looking forward to being discharged to clinic. And because the clinic is at the other end of the corridor, I exercised the little faith I had left by strolling down to the clinic to see people already going through clinic process. I was feeling encouraged that soon, I will be like these people, feel like them, and looking forward to coming to a clinic from my own house once a week. I also knew that being discharged to clinic brings its own issues and concerns, such as the possibility of complications and relapse. Although the fear was there, but the expectation of being well and fully cured of this disease was greater than the fears.

I was anxiously expecting restarting my life over again.

CHAPTER 7
SAVED AND SENT

"For by Grace I have been saved through faith, and that not of yourselves; it is the gift of God, not of works, lest anyone should boast" Eph. 2: 8-9

Finally, I was discharged from hospital ward to the clinic! Yippee! At first, I had to attend clinic twice a week but now I was back home and going to clinic from home. I was home eating everything but hospital food; I was now trying extremely hard to get my appetite back. My visits to the clinic were progressively rewarding because my recovery was progressively positive. It is important to say here that this was still a period of uncertainty because anything could happen. But my experiences during my stay at the hospital ward has galvanised an impassioned idea in me to support Cancer Research charities and set up a charity that will serve ethnic minority groups in particular. The idea included establishing a charity in Nigeria so it can really serve the people by providing education, awareness, diagnosis of cancer and where to get help. This idea was conceived based on my experience at the hospital that the ethnic minority groups are the group that least understood cancer. This group is the group that least understands the importance of donating blood or stem cell that can treat those who require transplant as the last resort for cancer treatment. Although I did not require transplant during the first episode of cancer, the doctors prepared for that just in case by conducting tests on my two siblings in case I needed it. My experience also opened my eyes to the fact that many cancer patients from ethnic minority backgrounds died needless deaths because of scarcity of cell donors amongst this group.

I was fortunate at the time that I did not require stem cell transplant as neither of my siblings matched. As I am now back home, I conducted online research to see if there was any such charitable organisation that has been set up to cater for this group of people. I discovered there were a few. One that was appropriately named the *African Caribbean Leukaemia Trust* (ACLT), and The *Anthony Nolan Trust*. The idea to establish a charity was conceived soon after I left hospital following the first cancer in 2006. Glory be to God that ten years later in early 2016, the process to establish and register *Forward Drive Health* began. By the special grace of God, a not-for profit organisation was set up in 2020.

I had knowledge of other patients who though discharged from clinic just before I was discharged were already having problems and complications.

This was scary as I worried that this may also happen to me, but glory to God that my clinical appointments, and subsequent consultations with doctors were moving progressively in the right direction. At the clinic were two wonderful nurses who got to know me from the ward and have been fantastic. These two ladies of African descent were professional to the core, caring, attentive and compassionate. Let me reiterate here that I value the nursing profession, especially within the National Health Service, for their dedication, compassion, commitment, understanding and care for patients. These are rare breeds who would leave their own problems at home and attend to their patients with utmost professionalism and dedication.

They are the backbone of the doctors or consultants because this group of people are the ones with daily and hourly interaction with the patients, whilst doctors come and go after examining the patients and prescribed needed drugs. The drugs are administered by the people in this noble profession called Nursing! I will talk more about nurses in the later part of this book.

Back to my attendance at the clinic. After I spent one month attending clinic from being discharged from the ward, the doctors were so pleased with my recovery and progress that my consultant asked if I could volunteer to act as patient liaison by going round the wards, talk to and encourage other patients who were on admission. The exact words of my consultant then were:

"David, you have been our most improved patient that we have had the privilege to look after in this ward. Your positive attitude to your treatment and your determination to beat cancer is unprecedented. We as doctors examine, based on our knowledge and skills, and prescribed drugs but we do not understand how you feel or what pains you go through during treatment. So, we would like you to volunteer, as much as your strength and energy can permit, to come into the wards for an hour on your clinic days and talk to patients and encourage as the Haematology Patient Liaison," (Consultant Haematology at Barnet General Hospital).

These words came through me like an arrow. I was literarily overwhelmed because truthfully, I did not understand how I survived the disease; although I remember every pain and anguish that I went through. I thought that it was a good idea. It would certainly make more impact if a fellow ex-patient such as myself talk to other patients undergoing treatment. I gladly agreed to take up this offer for two reasons: first to contribute positively towards helping other cancer patients because I have been saved by grace. I know personally how hard it is to live in that space, how hard it is to go through leukaemia. Secondly and selfishly, that I will wear one of those white overcoats and look like a consultant! Although I was excited about the prospect of interacting with patients and sharing my own experience and determination that got me out of the ward to the clinic, I also had the fear of what to expect but I remembered that *God has not given us a spirit of fear and timidity, but of power, love and self-discipline"*. (2 Timothy 1:7 NLT) and I prayed. Once I had this assurance, I could not wait to hit the wards and spread the story of courage and faith to the patients irrespective of their religious beliefs. I was not there to preach or impose my faith, I was going in there to share my story, to share my experience in the same wards where I had been for the eight months, to give encouragement and hope. Praise God! I was excited at the prospect of helping other patients to cope with their treatment, but I did not bargain nor expect the negative and emotional side-effect this would have on me. I started well even when I found it difficult to get through to some patients initially. This was because most patients thought I was a doctor at first especially with my white overcoat. Most of them wanted to be left alone as they think doctors do not understand what they were going through. Mind you, I was in that place at the start of my treatment too, so I understood. I remember three patients whom I will briefly highlight my experiences within this section. I am highlighting these three people because my experiences with them shaped my life and my thinking and I will not forget them.

The first patient I met was a middle-aged Nigerian male, about fifty-five (55) years old. He was admitted into Haematology Unit just a week after I was discharged from the ward, and he was in the same room that had been my room, my home for the last three months of my stay in hospital. The nurses explained his case to me he has refused to eat or take his drugs regularly; he was extremely upset that he has fallen victim to a foreign disease called cancer. I could not remember exactly what type of cancer it was that he had, but I recollect he was extremely hostile towards me when I entered his room. He was angry with the entire world. Mind you, I can relate to this because, I was in that place where I refused to accept that I had cancer. But unlike him, I did not take my frustration out on the nurses or doctors; I was also not as hostile to my environment as he was. I entered his room and politely explained my mission that I was there to spend some time with him and to encourage him. My message was that "being diagnosed with cancer does not mean death sentence." This was the motto I formed for myself at the early stages of my admission at hospital, and it worked for me. I remember the man angrily uttered the followings words to me: "*How can you possibly understand, you are not in my shoes, you do not understand what I am going through.*"

Wow! That was tough, believe me. I responded that I fully understood and that I am not a doctor, but a patient who has gone through the same process and pain during my treatment in this same ward for eight months prior, before being discharged recently to clinic. I went as far as telling him I spent the last three months of my hospital stay on the same bed where he was at. I showed him a few pictures of myself I took during my treatment, I call it my 'skeletal frame' photos, that I was carrying around as evidence and testimony. This worked magic, and we became good friends, he started taking his drugs and started developing a positive attitude towards his treatment. I visited him regularly until he was discharged after finishing his cycles of chemotherapy. I lost touch with him because he went back to Nigeria but at least I was happy that I changed his mind set, and I hope he is still alive today.

The second person I want to share her story is a younger lady of Ghanaian origin. The problem is that this lady was in the ward with me at the same time. And we were discharged to the clinic almost the same time. But less than two months in the clinic she had severe complications and a relapse, an incredibly sad case. The relapse did not come to me as a surprise because she really struggled for most of the time she was on admission in the ward. Incidentally, she needed to be admitted in the ward again for another round of chemotherapy treatment cycles. Relapse can occur in several ways during remission period. It is either the patient's body has refused to respond to treatment, or the cancer cells have quickly grown back again. Or a patient can have a relapse post remission period as it happened in my case. You will read about my 'Second-World-War' battle with leukaemia in the next few chapters. Either way, it is usually more dangerous, more aggressive, and sometimes terminal when one has a relapse. This is because the cancer cells are now attacking a weaker body with exceptionally low or non-existent immunity to fight the scourge.

Back to this lady, I was on my usual ward round to visit patients after my own clinic appointment as soon as I arrived the nurse at the Nursing Station told me I had to go to this lady's room and talk to her as she has refused to eat or drink all day. I rushed quickly to her room, which was just a few doors away from the Nursing Station. On entering her room, I was shocked with what I saw and heard; she looked so distant, her eyes shining like bright light bulbs, looking way beyond me into the distance. She was speaking in tongues basically, but she remembered who I was. Her last words to me were: *"David, I am going to rest, I cannot fight anymore because they are calling me".* I remember encouraging her not to listen to those inner voices and that she should be stronger, and that she would get through this. I prayed with her although I was the only one praying and saying amen to my own prayers. She was long gone away from me and from this world because her pupils were so shining it was scary. I did not know what to make of the experience, but I was glad that 'we' prayed together before I left.

She nodded and thanked me, asked me to go but make sure I came back to see her the next day. I did not know that was to dismiss me as she was ready to depart this sinful world leaving Cancer behind.

I was on my way home when I got a call from the Nurse that she had died! These were memories in my head which I can never forget, hence the birth for the idea behind this book. It is important for families to know and understand that cancer is a deadly disease and sufferers need support and understanding from those close to them. This woman probably gave up because throughout her stay in hospital, she did not have any close relative or friends visiting her to offer support and encouragement. Throughout our stay together in hospital, I had suspected that maybe she did not have anyone close by, or she did not really allow anyone into her world whilst in hospital. She may not have told anyone what she was going through. This is an attitude common to most Africans, who are often afraid to tell others about their situation during tough times, often due the myth of being bewitched!

The third and last patient I want to tell you about is the young twenty-four-year-old girl I mentioned earlier. She had loving parents, but she struggled through her cycle of chemotherapy treatments. I used to think that maybe it was because she was petite and had little energy to take all the aggressive chemotherapy dosages. But she was brave and pulled through her treatment after spending about eight months in the hospital. It was interesting to say that she found love through adversity. Her boyfriend then was a constant visitor who came to her bedside at the hospital daily. He went through it all with her and through the difficulties, their love grew stronger and they agreed to get married once she was out of hospital. Lo and behold, she was discharged into clinic not after I was discharged, so we continued to meet up at the clinic on days when our clinic appointments are set for the same day. She got married to her boyfriend as planned, soon as she was well enough to attend the ceremony. I lost touch with her after discharge from clinic, I later learnt that she died just months after getting married from aggressive secondary relapse leukaemia!

Although the stories above were sad because two of them eventually died from relapse leukaemia, the lesson here being that I am truly a living testimony today. I was in the same ward with many other patients in Barnet General Hospital, old and young; but some patients died because of shortage of matching bone marrow for transplant. The Ghanaian lady I mentioned above was one of them. The only option available for her to survive was a stem cell transplant, there was no blood or cell donor match from the ethnic minority groups hence her avoidable death.

For seven years up to 2013, I was in remission. I had regular hospital clinic appointments immediately after discharge from hospital ward to monitor my progress. At the beginning, it was weekly appointments, then monthly after two months, then quarterly and by 2008, I was having six-monthly appointments. In early 2008, I sought permission from my consultant to travel to Nigeria for two reasons. First, I was eager to travel to Nigeria because I never thought I will survive to see the country of my birth again, the second reason was to earn a living because at the time I left the hospital, getting a job in the United Kingdom, or getting back to where I was in my career pre-cancer was extremely difficult. It has been established that cancer or any related life-threatening disease affects not only patients physically; it affects emotionally and financially. For example, unless you are a multimillionaire, chances of getting employed after surviving cancer is usually very slim and permit me to say without prejudice, even more so when you are of African descent. The social security system is not the solution either, as the law is not so friendly to patients who recovered or survived cancer. Post-treatment remission period was a difficult time.

I went through many emotions which even the closest person to me (my wife) could not understand nor fathom. It is important to mention here as well that many things go through your mind when you have just left hospital, trying to get back to normal life. I will say more about this later. I was in remission from 2006 to 2013. Usually, it is five years but my consultants at Barnet Hospital (bless them) were gracious enough to keep seeing me for a further two years just to be sure I was free of the disease. Eventually, I was discharged fully in June 2013, and I was relieved because I thought that was to be the end of cancer in my life. How wrong could I have been!

CHAPTER 8
THE RELAPSE

"There are many plans in a man's heart, nevertheless the Lord's counsel – that will stand." Prov. 19:21

My plans after seven years in remission was to live life to the full and set up a charity to help other people going through cancer. However, God had other plans for me to fulfil His glory. There is a common saying that "lightning does not strike twice at the same place." But that was not entirely true in my case, because leukaemia did strike twice! Throughout the rest of 2013 and the first ten months of 2014, I was adjudged to have conquered cancer. Even though I was having some symptoms that got me worried, I did not want to accept that the cancer was back. I had fears at the back of my mind that I could not understand or explain to anyone, nonetheless, I was constantly praying silently that there would be no problem.

Something happened in October 2014 that got me terrified and it got my wife extremely worried too. We were at the First Baptist Church in Festac Town,

Lagos, Nigeria and during the service, I noticed I had a slight bruise on my wrist and was shocked to see blood dripping out of my veins. This development of a bruise and non-stop bleeding was a reminder of my first diagnosis some years back, and the worry I felt was that this is one of the main symptoms of leukaemia cancer. In the middle of the church service, my wife got up to get the first aid box, unfortunately none of the first aiders were at the 9am service. She had no choice but to fetch some toilet tissue paper to stop the bleeding. We had to leave church in the middle of the sermon because the bleeding did not stop. Prior to this, I have been experiencing other symptoms such as fatigue, tiredness, and chronic headache. The sudden bleeding that Sunday at the church brought home the fear that I had. What is this? Could this be just a normal routine of bleeding from a minor cut? Could this really be happening? Has the cancer come back? I was in denial, but the fear was there. At the back of my mind, I knew something was wrong, but I could not conclude what was becoming inevitable. Few days later, my wife contacted a medical doctor who had a diagnosis centre within the complex where we had our office in Lagos. I did not know that she was also worried and told the doctor to carry out a comprehensive analysis of my blood sample. I did not know she already told the doctor about my leukaemia experience. By this time, my wife was completing the project she was doing in Nigeria, and we were considering when we will move back to the

UK. The Doctor carried out physical examination and took numerous blood samples. We had to wait for a few days, and I was already very anxious when he came back on the third day with the results. He came over to our office, and my wife and I went into the inner office with him. As we sat down, he handed over the test results and uttered these words:

"Sir, I have never seen someone who survived this type of cancer until I met you. But, looking at these results, I will advise you to waste no time and get on the flight and quickly go back to where you were originally treated so you can get a comprehensive diagnosis."

His words came to me like a thunder, chilling and scary. This was early January 2015. The problem with cancer is that the person being diagnosed gets the shivers once the news break you may likely have cancer, again. It is an inner thing; it is the thing about cancer that makes it always appear so deadly. But it is important to say here that, it is better to know than not knowing, many people have died needlessly because they were too afraid to get tested and find out on time, by the time they found out they have cancer, it is too late because the cancer has reached an advanced stage. In the book of Hosea chapter 4:6, the first part says, *"My people are destroyed for lack of knowledge."* Early detection is key to survival. Without further delay, I started preparing to go back to the United Kingdom.

I arrived back in the UK early March 2015 and as soon as I could secure an appointment, I went to the GP surgery and a series of examinations, including blood, liver, and kidney function tests were carried out. I waited two weeks for the test result, which I understood was sent to Hertford Royal Infirmary Hospital for analysis. The GP requested that I undertake another blood test because the first round of tests was inconclusive. Inconclusive? Exactly what does that mean, I asked myself. I started panicking because this was confirming my worst fears that I might have a relapse, ten years after the first treatment! I did the second test and was sent to the Haematology consultant at Barnet General Hospital. A bone marrow biopsy was carried out to check for cancer cells and I recall that our family friend who was with me ran away from the waiting room as she could not stand the sound of pain from my treatment room. Following the Biopsy, I had an appointment at the hospital three days before I was due to fly back to Nigeria. I was a little apprehensive and anxious; when I arrived at the hospital, I was given papers for the usual blood tests and had other pre clinic checks such as blood pressure, weigh in etc before meeting with the consultant haematologist. I was well known at the Haematology department of Barnet General Hospital and I knew practically everybody. I was chatting with the lady at the reception desk when I was called in for consultation and the following conversations ensued:

Consultant: Hi David, what are you doing here again?

Me: Hello Doctor, I have no idea, but my General Practitioner insisted I see you

Consultant: Okay let us see (flipping through my medical records and looking at the large computer screen in front of her.

Me: I do not understand why I am back here when I was only released from the clinic a year or so ago. I am scheduled to fly back to Nigeria in three days' time.

At that moment, her expression was deadpan. Then the consultant looked up and said to me…

Consultant: Okay David. Go home and if I do not call you by 2 pm today, you can get on your flight back to Nigeria on Saturday!

I must confess that I knew something was wrong, but she wanted me to get home, in a comfortable environment, possibly with family and friends around me, before she gives me the news. I walked to the bus stop, I felt very weak, struggled to get on the bus and I slept throughout the journey from the hospital to my destination. My phone rang at exactly one minute to 1400 hours GMT. The caller's ID was "unknown", and I answered straight away and said, "*Yes, Sylvia.*" She asked how I knew it was her, but I was not ready for pleasantries. She asked me if I had people around me and I said yes, even though I was alone. My fears were all but confirmed when she said over the telephone the following words: "*David, I am sorry to tell you that the cancer has come back. You have been diagnosed with Secondary Relapsed Acute Myeloid Leukaemia*" This is the second time I would hear a similar '*I am sorry to tell you*' from doctors in ten years! Only this time around I did not know what to say. I have only heard of a few patients who had survived leukaemia once, never heard someone survived leukaemia twice so I did not think I had much hope, especially when she also told me in the same telephone conversation that I must prepare to get myself to University College London Hospital in a matter of three days whilst they get me a bed. The urgency of my admission to hospital was a major concern as I felt that the doctors were probably concerned about my chances for survival. I was afraid, but amid my fears, I remembered God's word "*But He was pierced for our transgressions, he was crushed for our iniquities; the punishment that brought us peace was on him, and by His stripes we are healed.*" (Isaiah 53:5). Even with these reassuring words, I would not say my fears disappeared completely, but at least it helped me to focus on God. I felt then that if God had wanted me dead, I would have died in Nigeria, when I was unwell and going through all those pain and discomfort. Although I was worried, I felt some reassurance.

I was staying with my adopted Christian brother at this time. He and his family took good care of me.... They took good care of me and I will forever be grateful for their generosity. During the period of my waiting between March and end of April for all the check-ups and tests results that I did, this family treated me so well I would have suffered more from the traumas I went through without them. They both worked full time, but the wife will always prepare my breakfast and lunch, wrapped the food up to keep warm before starting work. I appreciate the family so much, but I know God appreciates and loves them much more. Thank you so much for your kindness, for your love, for your prayers and for your wonderful support.

I will forever acknowledge the grace of God Almighty on my life, who answered my prayer and my cry for help. Now that the diagnosis has been confirmed as secondary relapsed Acute Myeloid Leukaemia, I asked God to heal me, so that I can be a *'Living Testimony'*. That was all I asked for, healing. Remember when God told Solomon to ask for whatever he needed to rule over God's children in Israel, Solomon asked for one thing, *Wisdom to rule according to God's way*! God responded to Solomon in II Chronicles 1:11 *"Because this was in your heart, and you have not asked riches or wealth or honour or the life of your enemies, nor have you asked long life—but have asked wisdom and knowledge for yourself, that you may judge My people over whom I have made you king---".* Solomon was endowed with so much wisdom than anyone on earth. At this stage I did not know what was ahead of me, how long was I going to stay in hospital? What type of treatment was this going to be? What kind of pains must I endure during the impending treatment?

I was ten years younger the first time I was diagnosed with leukaemia in 2005; my body function was more active. My immune system was stronger and able to recover quickly from aggressive chemotherapy. Even my intellect was stronger, my brain worked better because it was more active. But ten years later, my body is not so responsive, ten years older than the first time, and the whole feeling is not helped with the nagging realisation that my body MOT was a little out of date. So how did I come about being diagnosed again after ten long years of being in remission? I had many questions that I could not answer but the immediate thing was to get to University College London Hospital. I was devastated, I was afraid, I was unsure of the future. The truth is, I suddenly felt weaker and was suffering from a bigger type of fatigue. It was as if this latest news had weakened me much more than I could have imagined. The thought of going through all the process of treatment again, with no certainty of coming out this time (that was my natural human feeling), but not God's plan for me as I eventually came out again victorious. Looking back now, I do not know how I survived the treatment but let me just revisit some moments during the gruelling six months stay at University College London Hospital.

CHAPTER 9
A LIVING TESTIMONY

"Jesus Looked at them and said, With Man this is impossible, but with God all things are possible." *Matt 19:26.*

Three days after that scary telephone conversation with my consultant, comes the day I needed to get into hospital at central London. It was a rainy Saturday in Hertfordshire and I had to get to the hospital by 4pm. Tunde, my host promised to drop me at the hospital but had other commitments which were prearranged for that afternoon. We eventually left home for the hospital and got stuck in traffic for more than an hour; I have not seen such traffic in Hertfordshire for a long time and it was not apparent what caused it. I was not in a state of mind to bother myself about the traffic with everything going on in my mind. But glory to God that I remembered what Jesus Christ told his disciples in Mathew 19: 26[13]. My hope was raised because I knew that what looked impossible and unbelievable to me is very possible

---

[13] With men this is impossible but with God all things are possible

with God, hence my faith was strengthened. Praise God, we were next to a rail station, I got down from the car and took the train into London, with Tunde promising to bring my bag to the hospital to ensure I did not have to struggle with my overnight bag. Meanwhile, my wife had contacted her friend who lives in Amersham (Bedfordshire) to meet me at the hospital and provide moral support when I was checking into the hospital as she could not be there with me. Her friend, Bridget Gbemudu-Harvey got to University College London Hospital ahead of me, bless her! I eventually got into hospital much later than the time I was given. One particularly important lesson I learnt during the period of being hospitalised and receiving treatment is the positive support that families, friends, consultants, doctors, and nurses gave me. There were days when I did not appreciate any of that because I was too much into myself and thought the entire world was against me. I mean why on earth would I have been afflicted with this disease a second time?

On getting to the University College London Hospital in central London, the hospital accommodation was a self-contained room with its own toilet and shower for convenience, on the 13th floor of the Main Hospital Tower on Euston Road. The hospital facility was wonderfully comfortable, I consoled myself that this was to make me worry less about the enormity of what I was about to face - the effects, the uncertainty and the dangers of the treatment coupled with the unforeseen circumstances such as human errors and how my body would react to each stage of the treatment cycle. The admissions nurse was genuinely nice and understanding. She settled me in nicely, although I was too preoccupied in my mind to ask her any questions. But thank God that our family friend, Bridget, who was by my side at the request of my wife asked all the right questions. The nurse told me to eat and sleep for the night as the doctor will come in the morning before my treatment starts. Tunde had arrived to drop off my overnight bag and after a while my visitors and the nurse left, and I was on my own. I could not eat because I was not hungry; I could not pray; no word of prayer came to my mouth. I just laid there on my bed that night and looked up to heaven.

"I will lift up my eyes to the hills - from where cometh my help? My help cometh from the Lord, the Maker of heaven and earth" (Psalm 121:1–2).

At times like this, faith is often tested to the limit. I was asking several questions but to no one in particular; I was asking why I was here again, having to go through the pain of cancer treatment, ten long years after the first treatment. I remember asking myself many questions, where did I go wrong? My mind went back to those intervening ten years between 2006 to 2015 and I wondered what I did wrong to have brought this back again, but I had no answer. I blamed myself as I sought to understand what I did or did not do right, but I had no answer. I could not sleep as I sought to answers, so decided I would do the one thing that came to my mind, which was to pray. I felt that if I prayed, I might fall asleep because I needed something to take my mind off my worries. I needed an escape from myself, from this dream! I opened my mouth and prayed

"Jesus is the Lord of my life. Sickness and disease have no power over me. I am forgiven and free from SIN and GUILT. I am dead to sin and alive unto righteousness." Reading the word and praying brought relief to my emotional pain, and it looked like an antidote until I fell asleep that night. The next day, I found myself facing the reality of staying in the Haematology Ward on the 13th floor for the foreseeable future, not sure of the outcome of the treatment. Things were moving rather too quickly beyond what one could ordinarily imagine because immediately after breakfast, I had to go to the Macmillan Cancer Centre within the vicinity of the hospital to get an intravenous *Pick line* fixed in readiness for chemotherapy. I went through the preparatory procedures like I did ten years earlier at Barnet General. At the initial stages, I kept asking myself what was going to become of me. Was I going to survive this the second time? My room was a private room, facing the ever-busy Euston Road. I spent a lot of time at the window, looking out and watching the world go by while I was stuck in the room all day long, wondering if I was going to

survive and be able to go out there into the world again someday. Time goes very slowly during the day as I watched cars driving by, people moving about seemingly with no care in the world, watching everything going on down there on the streets. Reflectively, I knew these throngs of people out there cannot see me, they do not know what I was going through, neither could anyone of those people know what was going to happen to them as they go about their daily routines. It made me realise that God is truly awesome. He is omnipotent; Lord over-all, so much so that no one can reason Him out! I kept pondering to myself as I watched every activity going on down there, wondering whether that is how God, our father, watches us, seeing everything that we do.

God is good, all the time. Looking out at the window as I do every day, my faith grew stronger. I knew that there was every possibility I could survive this second cancer and come through, even though I have never heard of anyone surviving leukaemia twice. I also had people around me who were helping to lift my faith. You must understand when I tell you that this second treatment is much harder for me to take than the first. This was due to few reasons which are related to one another. The first reason is that I am now ten years older than when I had the first treatment and the older one gets with cancer treatment the harder it is to cope. Second, I was pessimistic and fearful about the treatment because

I know I survived the first time, but I was not sure about this second time, especially when I was told at diagnosis that I had to go into hospital for immediate admission, and treatment must start immediately. The doctors constantly mentioned that I might not survive it.

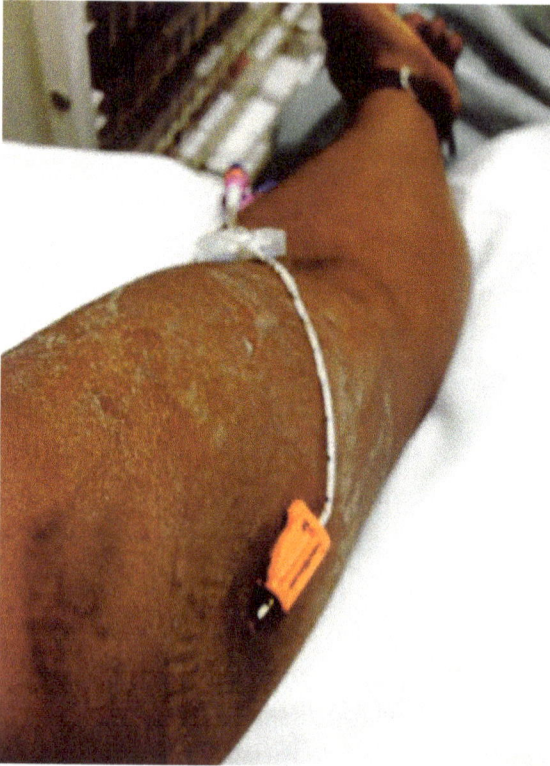

Pic 1: Pick line permanently inserted for intravenous treatment

However, there was a piece of good news in all of this. Treatment methods have advanced way beyond ten years ago. Medical research has advanced, more people are now surviving various types of cancer than before. I also realised that continuous prayer and praise will build the faith that will bring me deliverance, and to overcome this cancer the second time. I had to cultivate a climate of faith for healing around me. I had to cultivate a belief of God's peace around me.

"Peace I leave with you, my peace I give you. I do not give to you as the world gives. Do not let your heart be troubled and do not be afraid." (John 14:27).

How so soothing…
I felt hopeless a lot of times amid trials, so much so that many times I was not at peace with myself. I needed to create that peace within me, hence the relevance of the second part of the scriptures above that I should not allow my heart to be troubled.

Phil 4: 7 also says *"And the peace of God, which transcends all understanding, will guard your hearts and your mind in Christ Jesus"*.

I realise that I have a battle on my hand, but I also have God's promises in abundance for me to go on. I had to believe that I shall once overcome again. I prayed there and then that my "case was going to be different!" I may not have known someone who survived leukaemia once, never mind twice. I have heard of important public figures, celebrities, from every race dying from the disease, but I knew that "Nothing is impossible with God". I started confessing that "I AM GOING TO BEAT THIS AGAIN AND BECOME A LIVING TESTIMONY". With the bullish attitude that I had cultivated, and my positive confessional statements, it was easier for me to embark on yet another long tenancy at the Haematology Ward on the 13th floor of the Main Tower at the University College London Hospital ".

CHAPTER 10
PEACE IN THE MIDST OF STORM

"I have told you these things, so that in me you may have peace. In this world you will have trouble. But take heart! I have overcome the world." John 16:33 (NIV)

I was in the Haematology ward at the main tower for the first round of treatment which lasted for eight weeks. This included two weeks during which I could go home to recuperate. The period spent at home was also a little traumatic because I was staying with my friend as our own house was occupied at the time. As the saying goes, "Man proposes, God disposes". We have rented out our house as we were working abroad for a few years. During my time out of hospital for recuperation after the first course of treatment, I stayed with our friend waiting for my wife and daughter to return from Nigeria, they got back to the UK before I returned to the hospital. Returning to the hospital after the first course of chemotherapy, I was admitted into the first floor of the main tower just for a few days, before my doctors recommended that I would better be looked after through the Ambulatory Care Services.

I have heard nothing about Ambulatory Care prior to this. I was worried at first because it sounded like Ambulance Care services. So many things were running through my head. I was asking myself if these doctors knew something I did not know; was I going to be treated inside an ambulance? What exactly is 'Ambulatory Care'? What was I to expect? I was too scared to ask further questions about this because it took my mind back to the first report of how the stem cell transplant treatment was going to be like. I was reminded of all the facts reeled off by one of the consulting doctor's when he met with my wife and me. We were told of what could happen during my treatment: that I might die from such things as 'Graft Versus Host Disease' (what is that?); or have they concluded that I may die from simple complications of chemotherapy treatment? Is that why they want me to go through "Ambulatory" or Ambulance Care? I kept wondering, and wildly too… it is with great relief when I found out what Ambulatory Care was, and what it meant to me receiving quality healthcare in a comfortable environment, which helped my treatment and recovery better.

"The University College London Hospital (UCLH) Ambulatory Care (AC) service delivers a range of treatments which have historically been administered

within the inpatient setting. Eligible patients receive their care in the Ambulatory Care Clinic area within the Cancer Centre and, if well enough, live in a local hotel with or without a companion, rather than in the hospital. If appropriate, patients may continue their treatment at home. If patients require hospital admission during their treatment, contingency beds are available 24 hours a day on our associated cancer wards." (Source: UCLH). Praise God.

To my surprise, Ambulatory Care Services can be described as a '5-Star' cancer treatment centre. Once I knew I was to receive treatment from Ambulatory Care Services, the first surprise I had was to be told I would leave the hospital ward to be lodged into a hospital accommodation for ambulatory care patients at Cotton Rooms right behind the main Macmillan Cancer Centre. At the Cotton Rooms, I had a wonderfully comfortable hotel room, a common living area for the patients and an expansive dining area where I can get something to eat literarily all day and all night long. There is also a proactive reception area staffed with competent and caring staff. This is heaven, I thought! My family could visit or stay with me anytime they chose thereby providing emotional support to get through the treatment regime. There were no restrictions on visiting times as family and friends could come any time. This was such great relief because at the hospital ward, you do not always have people to talk to about your feelings or treatment. Many nights at the hospital ward, I laid in bed writhing in severe pains, and naturally unable to sleep. Sometimes I worried that if I close my eyes and sleep, I might never wake up. There was fear, anxiety, and uncertainty when alone at the hospital. It was still there even at the Ambulatory Care Services, but the difference is that now I had access to my family support twenty-four-seven with no worries. Occasionally, when my wife and daughter slept over and stayed with me, I had so much peace of mind even amid the worries and fear. I felt that even if I was going to die, at least my family will be there for me to say my goodbyes, until we meet at the foot of Jesus, to part no more. This is so true that there is no substitute to family support when going through cancer treatment. It made me feel I was not alone, it made me realise that I had been selfish and angry at the entire world, including them (my family), because I did not think I deserve to be where I was at the time. I did not think I deserve to suffer this pain again the second time in ten years.

It was easier to leave the Cotton Rooms accommodation and take five minutes' walk down to the Cancer Centre for my daily treatment, which was like three times a day. A few of my friends came to the 'comfortable' hospital accommodation to see me. God showed me that I was surrounded by wonderful family and friends who cared a lot about me. Some of my professional colleagues became my best friends through their care and concern for my health and wellbeing. I remember that my long-term friends and professional colleagues, Wale, Julius and Oyewole came to see me and we had banters which were a source of energy to me. I must express my gratitude to Oyewole especially, who, at different times, will carry boxes of water up several flights of stairs to t my Cotton Room accommodation! That was no mean feat. I appreciate all my family and friends much better after undergoing cancer treatment the second time. The transfer of my treatment to the ambulatory care was after the completion of the first cycle of a planned two-cycle chemotherapy treatment. And the transfer to ambulatory was necessitated with the near certainty that I would have to go through stem cell transplant as the final treatment for this disease. Prior to the planning of the stem cell treatment procedures, my wife and I were invited to see the stem cell transplant consultant for another pre-treatment review. A lot of what the doctor said to us at that review meeting were scary to say the least. I was told I had series of problems during the first course of chemotherapy treatment I had just completed; problems with SEPSIS, particularly with the FLA_IDA drug; and a fungal chest infection. As if these were not enough problems to think about, the doctor went ahead to give a graphic account of possible adverse effects that can happen because of pressing ahead with the stem cell transplant at the time. Sometimes you listen to these consultants with so much negative effect of treatments you wonder if it was ever necessary. We went through the rationale for proceeding with haploidentical reduced intensity transplant, which would involve more chemotherapy and radiotherapy. There were all sorts of potential complications such as Graft versus host disease, possibility of organ toxicity with lung, liver, cardiac, renal toxicity, and bacterial and fungal infections! There was also the risk of mucositis, and that I may get some haemorrhagic cystitis. Wow, all these problems possible from a treatment that is meant to solve the whole leukaemia problems! But guess what, that is where God's word comes in as in Proverbs 3: 5 *"Trust in the LORD with all thine heart; and lean not unto thine own understanding"*. Mind you I did not have any understanding of all the medical jargons I have listened to for the past hour, but I understand God's promises and the healing power of the saviour Jesus Christ. That was more than enough comfort for me at such difficult time.

There were milestone testimonies during my stay at Ambulatory Care and living at the Cotton Rooms hospital accommodation, but the importance of family and supporters around me during that treatment was paramount. My condition got worse one evening to the extent that I was scared the end had come. I was in serious pains more than I had ever experienced since my treatment began. My wife and eight-year-old daughter did everything they could to help me ease the pain; we prayed, they told jokes and told stories all in an attempt for me to feel relieved, but it was like nothing worked. They did not understand what was happening. But how could they when I did not even understand what was happening to my own body and person? I could not understand the sudden deterioration in my condition, I tried to rationalise it, but I had no relieve nor an immediate answer. This went on through the night and I could have had less than two hours sleep all night; the pain was unbearable. The next morning, my wife took me to the Ambulatory Care Services at the Cancer Centre about two hundred yards away. The nurse on duty sat me down and fixed me on intravenous and gave me two bags of what I thought at the time was a powerful drug because of the speed of which my energy came back and the pain receded. I asked the nurse the name of the drug I was given that was so strong and effective as to have released me from a twelve-hour misery so fast. And she told me it was 'just water'. Ordinary water? Can you imagine that? Just water! Do you mean to tell me that I went through twelve hours of discomfort just because I did not drink enough water? She said in the affirmative, "David, you have been advised to drink plenty of water to relieve the effect of chemotherapy drugs, but you did not take our advice!" This was a great lesson for me to realise the effect of the chemical H_2O (water), even though I learnt about this in the science class during my secondary school days.

This was a great lesson learnt, and that which I would wish to pass on. Water a powerful medication for all kinds of diseases that our body may encounter as we cruise through our daily lives because it flows through the body system and help to flush the clogs in the system to enable free flow of blood through the veins. The British Society for Cell Biology describes water as *"the single most abundant chemical found in living things and cells"*. So that says it all, the power of water. We take things like drinking water for granted because we are surrounded by all the chemicals on the store shelves to pollute our body even further. Thank God for all His provisions, and for the provision of water.

CHAPTER 11
NEW CELLS, NEW LIFE

"You have power over your mind – not outside events. Realise this, and you will find strength."

Marcus Aurelius, Roman Emperor from 161 to 180 and a stoic philosopher

How much I needed to find strength and feel courage at this crucial stage of my treatment. This was the period of destiny, the period that determines whether the planned stem cell transfer will work. What would the feeling be growing new cells? Am I going to change physically and become a new man? Do I have the power over my mind right now? Many kindergartens' questions were coming to my mind, and I felt like I was having a combination of mental and emotional meltdown. I sure did not have power over my mind right now because it is easier said than done. But I had to muster the strength to control the battle going on in my mind. The medical team had put in place a comprehensive programme for stem cell transplant as the last option to cleanse me of the cancer. I have had full counselling on the process and the expectations. The process for the transfer began six weeks earlier when my brother who had agreed to donate his stem cells came England for a few weeks to enable him to undergo the preparatory tests. During this period, he was given medication to build his cells up to an appropriate level required for the process of transfer to succeed. The picture below shows my brother during the process of stem cells collection for the imminent stem cell transplant. The tough part of the process was the numbers of hours he needed to lie in bed for the collection, it lasted eight hours but it seemed like a lifetime. I did not foresee such lengthy process for my brother who was donating, which made me wonder how long the process of transfer was going to take. I later understood that the process of stem cell transplant had to be well planned to avoid possible complications at every stage of the process. The treatment process was called 'Reduced Intensity Haplo.' The stem cell programme lasted from the 14th to the 27th of August 2015, with the actual transfer occurring on the 21st, meaning there were seven days before and seven days after the actual transfer. I was still at the hospital accommodation at the Cotton Rooms for the preceding seven days to the transplant on the 21st day of the August but moved to the main ward of the hospital for the radiotherapy and stem cell transplant. These were uncertain and challenging times. Despite the planning that has gone into cell infusion programme, my anxiety level for the outcome of the procedure was high. My daughter and wife were with me on the first day of the infusion programme. I remember willing myself to be strong and not showing the doubts and fear, but really, I was not fooling either of them. It came to a point that my daughter became so distressed and she was just telling the doctors and nurses around, *"Please do not let my Daddy die!"*

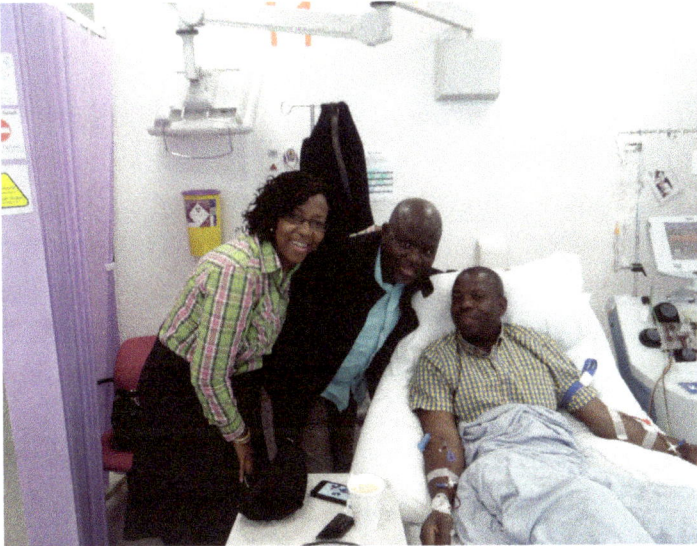

Pic 2: My wife and I observing the cell donor procedure

That was so hard to take, seeing a child so distressed about her father's condition and expressing anxiety in such a way. Seeing this, I realised I must dig deep into my inner self and be strong. With my daughter being in distress and to see the state she was in, God moved miraculously to send her away on a month holiday in Canada. My wife told me that her brother Francis, who lives in Canada, has sent a ticket to our daughter so she can be away from the environment at such critical stage of my treatment. This could not have come at a better time because it was best for her to be away. She did not to see me in a continuous helpless state like this, but I was also apprehensive because this may be the last time that I see my daughter if the stem cell transplant did not work. That is how wonderful our God is. He gets His people out of impossible situations for His glory.

With my daughter away on a glorious holiday, all attention and prayers now switched to the next few days for the stem cell infusion programme. I had to go through several tests, minor preparatory operations, several ECG scans, with appointments literarily every two hours for several days to go for tests, yet more tests at different clinics of the hospital. The diagram below shows the timetable of the treatment, and the different drugs administration over the period of the stem cell transplantation. The consultant presented me with this timetable, and I was not sure what to think. It was surprising the amount and types of drugs I must take before, during and after the cell transfer date. I had consultation with doctor's verbally and information was put in writing. The consultation included the benefits and the attendant implications of the process. It is the normal practice for doctors to provide information to the patient about treatment; and I can tell you that, as usual, the prognosis was not good. I cannot post the assessment letter that I received here because it is so grim and looks more like a signpost for lost hope. But I remember that during the night of minus Day 7 above, I could not sleep thinking of what could happen at this late stage. I kept pondering about what the doctors have told me about my chances for survival or otherwise; the uncertainty, anxiety on the risk of catching "Graft Versus Host Disease". Believe me, I did not understand what that meant, despite all the explanations! So much to consider, so much to process with so much to digest. Lord have mercy!

Suddenly the thought of the control tower and the airplane pilot I mentioned earlier came through to me. I felt like I was already a passenger in an airplane that has just taken off from the departure terminal and the airplane is airborne. I thought now the airplane is airborne. I was powerless and cannot come down from the airplane even though I was feeling sick. The pilot would not turn the airplane around just because of me. I am stuck here in the airplane, with the belief that the airplane will land safely at the set destination! My destination here being complete healing and full recovery from leukaemia. All I can do now is rest on God

"When you pass through the waters, I will be with you; and when you pass through the rivers, they will not sweep over you. When you walk through the fire, you will not be burned; the flames will not set you ablaze." (Isaiah 43:2)

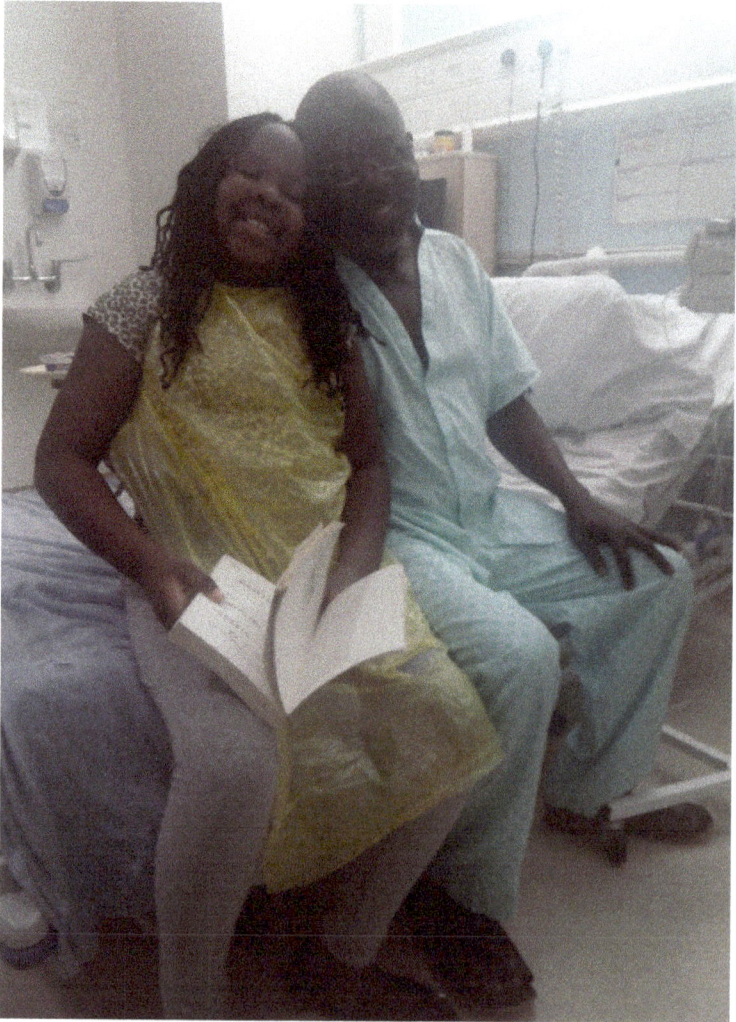

Pic 3: Family support, my daughter support was crucial

	Date	Details
-7	Fri, 14/08/15	ADMIT
-6	Sat, 15/08/15	FLUDARABINE CYCLOPHOSPHAMIDE
-5	Sun, 16/08/15	FLUDARABINE CYCLOPHOSPHAMIDE
-4	Mon, 17/08/15	FLUDARABINE
-3	Tue, 18/08/15	FLUDARABINE
-2	Wed, 19/08/15	FLUDARABINE
-1	Thu, 20/08/15	2 Gy TBI
0	Fri, 21/08/2015	STEM CELL INFUSION
+1	Sat, 22/08/15	REST DAY
+2	Sun, 23/08/15	REST DAY
+3	Mon, 24/08/15	CYCLOPHOSPHAMIDE to start 60-72 hrs after stem cell infusi
+4	Tue, 25/08/15	CYCLOPHOSPHAMIDE
+5	Wed, 26/08/15	START TACROLIMUS MMF TILL D +30
+6	Thu, 27/08/15	START G-CSF

University College London Hospitals NHS

Haemopoietic Stem Cell Transplantation Programme

NAME: David Fadipe   DOB:

HOSPITAL NUMBER: 40032553

DIAGNOSIS: AML

TREATMENT: REDUCED INTENSITY HAPLO

Programme for the Cell Transfer

DAY OF RECKONING

"I shall not die but live, so that I can proclaim the glory of the Lord." Ps 118:17

What blessed assurance! It is refreshing to say that God's word provides us with answers in every situation; whether at crossroads, hopelessness or helplessness, God starts with us where we stop to heal through his words. I struggled with whether to write just my experiences from the world perspective and let everyone read it or tell my story from the perspective of the miraculous healing and God's mercy had upon my life. The second reason got the better of me to write this experience in line with my faith in God for my healing, most especially because my entire experience was just one big miracle. I have met with other patients during post-treatment advocacies with Cancer Research UK and Macmillan Cancer Care who have survived various types of cancer in the past. Some have cancer treatment for years before being cured, but I am yet to meet any surviving patient of leukaemia who have survived twice. I choose therefore, to declare the glory, grace, and mercies of God over my life, as in the words of the Psalmist above.

I will never forget the day I went to Radiology clinic for a full body radiation treatment. The department was located two floors down at the basement of the hospital. Though I had been told that it was going to be difficult, but I did not expect what I got, because the experience was probably one of my scariest of treatments at Macmillan Cancer Centre. I got into the clinic with my wife and the Radiographer marked spots on my body to highlight the parts to be targeted for radiation and my arms and legs were folded and I was strapped up ready for the radiation treatment. I was told to lie still during the treatment which lasted for 90 minutes, split into two halves of 45 minutes. I was asked to turn my body over to the other side at the interval period. The hard part was that I had to maintain the same position for the entire period to get adequate radiation result. I was worried that if I needed to go to the toilet, what will I do?

I took my mind off completely from the distracting thought and was lucky to make it to the end of the period. By the time the process was completed I was unstrapped from the equipment, I tried to get up, but my feet were completely numb. The Radiotherapist assisted me as I was expectedly breathless, weak, and unable to stand. Assisted by my wife, I stay seated for a while and I drank plenty of water before I could stand upright. In it all, God was with me and His word came to me as a soothing relief after a very hectic day. *"The Lord your God is with you, the Mighty Warrior who saves. He will take great delight in you, in His love He will no longer rebuke you, but will rejoice over you with singing."* (Zephaniah 3:17). The words were so appropriate because there was always uncertainty and fear at every stage of the treatment, even after the stem cell transplant. I had to hold firm God's assurance, that the Mighty Warrior who saves will rejoice over me. Hallelujah.

I have now entered the stem cell transfer cycle stage, and it was to take fifteen days (minus day 7 to day one, and seven more days after transfer). I had seven days of intense preparation taking various drugs and bucket full of water on a regular basis. It was like a soldier preparing for war. I needed to be fully hydrated to allow the drugs to settle with no adverse effect. The process of infusion itself was simple and lasted for two hours, I laid down wondering what was happening to me, how was this supposed to be the "saving blood" that I needed to beat this disease? What happens now? How long was it going to take before these new blood cells kicks in and take away this pain? Was I going to look like a different person? Was I losing my mind? Would I be the same person again? I felt nothing whilst the infusion was going on, I was just lying down with many funny thoughts going through my mind.

"Many are the plans in a person's heart, but it is the Lord purpose that will stand." Proverbs 19:21.

A couple of days after the stem cell infusion were rest days: no medication, no doctors nor clinic attendance, just the normal routine nurses' check-up and plenty of rest. Believe me, I needed those two days' rest after everything I had gone through pre-transplant. But despite the resting, I was anxious because these were crucial stages of the transplant working or not working, with monitoring of my weight, blood count, heart rate and platelet counts.

I understood then that the rest period was to allow the stem infusion to settle into the bloodstream. But it was more nerve-racking because it was also a period of uncertainty, anxiety, and fear all rolled into one. Cautiously optimistic with hope, I was aware of the possibility that my body may reject the cells. I nothing to hope for should that happens. According to the medical personnel, stem cell transplant was the last option for treatment. I knew that having gone this far my God would not leave me now. I rested well in the assurance that my hope lies in God's hands. Sleeping was easy as I literarily slept throughout the two days with no problem. My sleeping was constantly disturbed by the flurry of visitors on those two days, but it was good having people around me immediately after my transplant. I have repeatedly said that family is key to my recovery; you need your family around you at those crucial times. Not just to be there with you, but to be understanding and to appreciate what you are going through. I found that little things were getting me upset very quickly but I had to accept the fact that I was where I was, and it was not due to nobody's fault. I was mindful of the fact that nobody knows or understand what you go through unless it happens to them!

The two days of rest came and went, and I started taking medications to help with assimilating the new cells into my system. Apart from the timetable of medication in the table above, the following two weeks after stem cell infusion was a beehive of activities. I was booked into different clinics of the hospital for different tests, including Hepatology, full body radiation and heart function tests. I had my blood taken like five to six times a day, so much so that it got me worried but was assured this is normal for regular monitoring and was necessary to see how the new cells were progressing.

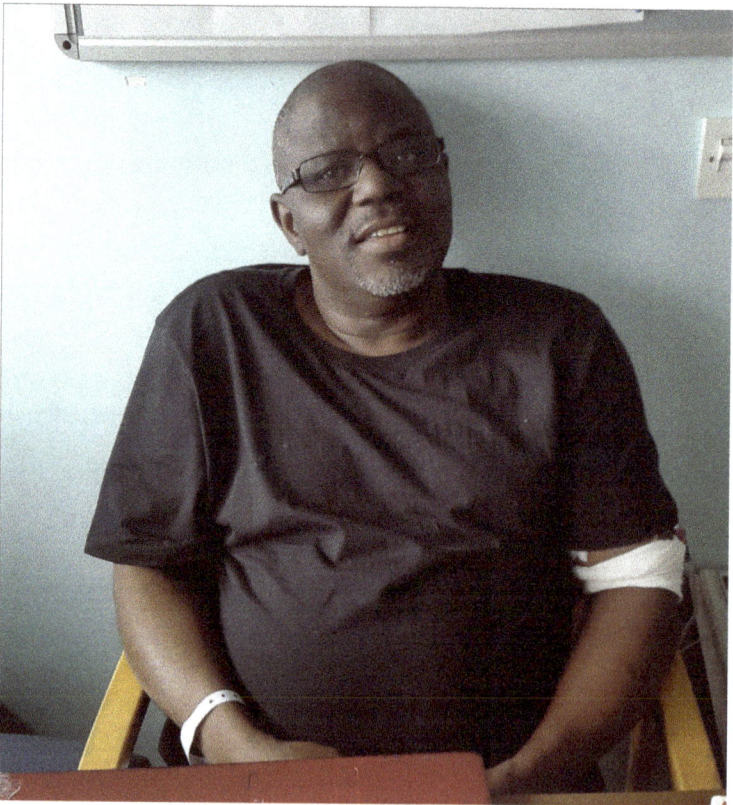

Pic 4: Exhausted; post-Transplant but still smiling

CHAPTER 12
HEALTH IS WEALTH

"And we know that all things work together for good to those who love God and are called according to His purpose." Romans 8: 28

Now that I have completed the stem cell transfer process, it was time for me to get back to the questions in my head during the heady days of preparing for the transplant.

What does the future hold for me after transplant? Am I strong enough for this treatment, especially after five months of intensive chemotherapy treatment that has battered my system? Will the transplant work? How do I deal with frustration about being in isolation during recovery? Do I have control over what happens to me during and after transplant? Was I going to die, despite the efforts of the nurses and the doctors? What happens to my family? It was quite easy to say this was a period of endless questions and worries for me and it lingered on before, during and post transplantation. Only the grace of God got me through all that, and here I am today, being a *Living Testimony*.

Let me quickly drop something here. I am writing this book for a few reasons: to share my experience in my own words but above all to show the goodness of God in my life, to return the praise and glory where it belongs, to God Almighty. He will not share His glory with anyone. He is Lord over all; He is the beginning and the end, the first and the last, the El Shaddai, the Ancient of days, Jehovah Sharma, Jehovah Elohim, there is none compared to our God, either in Heaven or on earth. Despite the stress of life sometimes, I wake up every morning and give Him the Glory and praise that are due only to Him. Praise God! It is important to say that the rest of my recovery from stem cell transplantation was smoother than I thought. The pains receded; the new cells harmoniously settled in with my body and praise God, there was no cell rejection. The beautiful thing was that my miraculous recovery and healing was an evangelism tool around the hospital. It was refreshing to see nurses, doctors and hospital workers coming to listen to my gospel music, which I played all day long to remind me of God's goodness in my life. I was amazed to see that there were lots of Bible-believing men and women in the medical field, from different races, colour, and creed. By His blood I am saved, By His blood I am healed, the blood was my covering, the blood of Jesus truly set me free from cancer. I was encouraged to the point where prayer for my healing was never in short supply day and night. My faith was renewed to see different people not being afraid to proclaim their faith and belief in God. I was discharged from hospital accommodation at Cotton Rooms and admitted back to the hospital room on the very day that I had radiotherapy and subsequently stem cell transplant because of the need for post-transplant care and monitoring in the hospital ward.

One other important thing to mention is that I received probably the best care and attention at the University College London Hospital and the Macmillan Cancer Centre. I really thank all the medical staff, doctors, and nurses for giving me a second (or shall I say third) chance to live. Here I was with new blood cells in my system, many doubts remain whether it will work, with fear of the unknown creeping in and out of my mind. When I was preparing for my transplant, I was pulled along at such a fast pace, going from clinic to clinic, having one test after another, blood samples after blood samples; so much so that I did not have time to worry about the consequences of cell rejection, nor possible infection of *Graft Versus Host Disease* (GvHD). By way of a quick explanation, '*Graft*' means my donor cells from my brother, which will form part of my new blood and immune system. Scary thought in every situation, is it not? But what choice do I have? I was just grateful to God for the opportunity to have those lifesaving donor cells. Throughout the process, I was cautiously optimistic and prayerful with God's word as my battle cry. *"Heal me Oh Lord and I shall be healed; Save me, and I shall be saved"* (Jeremiah 17:14). I have no control over my body accepting the new stem cell, nor do I have control over infection for Graft Versus Host Disease or any other adverse reactions already highlighted by medical personnel in charge of my treatment, but I had control over my ability to dwell in God's word and trust in it to be true. The good news is that I found through research that some Graft versus Host Disease (GvHD) can be a good thing because it means that my new blood and immune system is working and will probably attack any remaining or returning cancer cells, a very encouraging sign to focus on the positives was to turn out as my testimony. Yes, I am a *"living testimony"*

THE STORM IS NEARLY OVER, HALLELUYAH

"Give Thanks to the Lord and proclaim His greatness." Psalm 105: 1.

The following weeks that I spent going through recovery appeared to drag slowly, so much so that it looked like a lifetime of recuperation. I was anxious, why won't I be? I was praying (yes), hoping (yes), and waiting (yes), but anxious at the same time. I thought I was used to the waiting game after each cycle of chemotherapy, but it was more difficult to get used to the anxiety from waiting and difficult to process the battle going on in my mind. There was nothing to do but to pray, hope and wait! I kept telling myself *"Do not be anxious or worried about anything, but in everything [every circumstances and situation] by prayer and petition with thanksgiving, continue to make your [specific] requests known to God"* (Phil 4:6 Amplified).

The beauty of God's word is that IT IS THE TRUTH, THE WHOLE TRUTH, AND NOTHING BUT THE TRUTH; the only requirements being 'believing' and 'obedience'.

The waiting days were not as bad as expected because there was optimism and hope with each passing day. Coupled with endless visitors of families and friends, this period of waiting was probably the busiest of visiting different clinics of the hospital, the Hepatology, Physiotherapy, and Respiratory clinics. Days rolled into nights and nights back into days, and the waiting continued. The good news however is that my recovery was progressing well. There was no GvHD or any of the other adverse reactions to my stem cell transplant as were previously predicted. Praise God Almighty! By the end of October 2015, I was discharged from hospital and went home.

The day of discharge was strange because I have become accustomed to the daily routine in the hospital environment against my best intentions.

Now, tell me that is not strange! But I was also a little apprehensive about my health outside of the hospital ward. Would I be okay? Was that it? I thought that the whole thing about life felt strange, confirming the feeling that the difference between living and dying is just but a single minute. The last visitor to come see me in the hospital were the couple from our Life Church family in Cuffley, Derek & Mary Gregory, bless them. It was really refreshing that they came around just before I left the hospital bed. We prayed together and just like it is said in the latter part of James 5:16 *".... The prayer of the righteous person is powerful and effective"* (*"the prayer of the Saints availed much"* in the KJV version).

I was discharged at about 11am in the morning and went home with my wife in an hospital-arranged transportation, and I was convinced that assuredly, I will be a 'living testimony' because I believed my healing was total and complete.

DO CHRISTIANS JUDGE?

Inadvertently YES! This is a controversial question to ask especially when you are writing a book to share your leukaemia experience and hoping that your experience impacts on people's life positively, and within the context of God's word which says: *"Judge not, and you will not be judged. Condemn not, and you will not be condemned. Forgive, and you will be forgiven.*" (Luke 6: 37). Let me be state briefly: "People will never truly understand something until it happens to them". You can never understand being without money to meet even the basic needs if you come from a rich background, especially if the riches have been effectively managed. Neither can you understand the feelings and sufferings of a cancer patient unless you were close to the patient, or you have suffered a life-threatening illness yourself.

This premise is even more reflective of us Christian folks because our perceptions and reactions of events happening around us can sometimes be because of our ignorance. YES! Christians can be ignorant especially when it comes to passing judgements on people facing difficulties. I have had some milestone challenges in my life, and it is the people within my Christian family that questioned my commitment to my faith and prayer. We live within this sinful world with all its problems and blessings and we, as Christians are not immune from the problems nor the environment that we live in. I decided to add this bit about Christian behaviours and reactions as a form of insightful message to others who face difficult situations of life, especially amongst the *self-acclaimed* charismatic Christians. Surely, we read the Bible very well, but we ignorantly pick certain parts of it that boost our ego and make us appear holier than we realistically are in certain situations. Christian brothers and sisters visited me in hospital, and some made comments that questioned my faith in God.

"Brother David, are you praying enough? Because Bible say that *'no evil shall befall you, neither shall any plague come near your dwelling'*. (Psalm 91:10*)* But they forgot another message of the Bible that says, *"He was wounded for our affirmatives by His stripes we are healed" (Isaiah 53:5)!* Sure, it was hard to understand the rationale behind a Christian family thinking this way. But I realised that culture and religious beliefs can be interwoven at times, especially amongst the black and minority ethnic groups. Dare I say that we interpret the Bible to suit our cultural heritage, I have witnessed so many pronouncements over the years about how we should be as Christians; look holy, act holy, pretend to be holy whereas we are anything but holy. The truth be told sometimes that people have the feeling that if you are going through some suffering, it is because you are not praying enough; or you have sinned, or its misfortune brought about as your action! But four years and a bit after discharge from hospital, I can confidently join the saying of the Psalmist that *"The stone which the builders rejected, has become the chief cornerstone";* and *"This is the Lord's doing. It is marvellous in our eyes". (Ps 118: 22-23).*

Evidently, I am not the same person I used to be prior to my experience with cancer, which was a bit of a problem for me immediately after transplant.

I remember that although I looked okay from the outside, everyone assumed that I was back to my old self even though during the initial months after transplant, I was carrying around a bag with intravenous fluid fed through my pick line to build up my immune system. Several questions kept running in my mind even at this period. For example, I was still in doubt as to whether I am healed of leukaemia! Is the stem cell transplant really going to work? As described in Joyce Meyer's book, '*Battlefields of the Mind*', I was engaged in a serious 'battlefield' within me. I had to admit that the whole thing experience seems unreal to me. My testimony in this book is a pivotal part of the unlimited favour and grace of God that I enjoyed which healed me of cancer, the dreaded Acute Myeloid Leukaemia (AML) twice in ten years! I do not take this lightly but with everything pointing to the fact that I am once again an overcomer, the battle has been the Lords and as His child I make no apologies to boast about His grace and mighty hand over me to this point.

It is crazy, it is unreal, but that is me thinking as a human for God's word seem to be coming true in my life and I probably did not see that happening because I was focussing on what the enemy, the devil, wants me to focus on. Whereas God's word has consistently confirmed to me that *"With men it is impossible, but with God all things are possible" (Mark 10: 27b)*. It has taken me nearly five years after treatment to complete the writing of this book. Probably because other things in life took my attention or because there were more revelations of God's goodness in my life during my many clinical appointments to the hospital in the aftermath of my treatment that God wanted me to add to the book. But it has been God all the way, there is no other explanation. Many times, I look at myself and I marvel at the God that I serve. I had my fears, but all those fears have been unfounded, because with each clinical visit to the Haematology Ward, my healing has been progressive to the amazement of medical experts. So truly, I am a LIVING TESTIMONY after all! Glory to God.

CHAPTER 13
THE AFTERMATH

"For whatever is born of God overcomes the world. And this the victory that has overcome the world – our faith" 1 John 5:4

This is the aftermath; Glory be to God. I have overcome cancer twice, trampled cancer under my foot twice in ten years. So, what is next? Treatment and survival of cancer may be one thing, but more challenging is getting back to a position where one can live through the aftermath of the treatment. I have been writing this book since I left hospital five years ago. It has been tasking, and I had almost given up lots of times due to fatigue, lack of interest, and experiencing bouts of depression caused by remembering the leukaemia treatment. Putting down my experiences in writing has not been easy. There are times when I have had flashbacks of my near-death experiences and panics had set in. These have been my experiences and feelings in the aftermath of going through cancer and surviving, it is easy to conclude that one never really get over having cancer fully, because the emotional feeling remains. I have had to guard my thoughts and my mind that this is the lie of the devil, because the Bible is clear in Isaiah 40:29 that *"He gives power to the weak, and to those who have no might He increases strength"*.

I am free of cancer despite any contrary story the enemy wants me to believe, and he whom the Son has set free, is free indeed. Please be careful and be aware of the devices of the enemy when contrary thoughts come to your mind against the plan of God for you. Remember *"we fight not against flesh and blood but against principalities and powers in the heavenly places"*. *(Ephesians 6: 12)* So, be vigilant, for the enemy is real, either within or without.

I have gone through bouts of depression a couple of times since leaving hospital but that is not down to just the cancer itself. It could be said that there are other contributing factors, and these are in a legion. What of the inability to get back to economic status pre-cancer? Unemployment played a part, so did low self-esteem and the fear of the unknown.

These are genuine issues but in it all, God has promised us his grace and blessings. I had successes during the ten-year intervening period between the two leukaemia experiences I have had in life. God has been good to me and I am here today proclaiming myself as a living testimony to the glory of God. Looking back, the successes that God gave me in doing what I love doing at a higher level took my mind away from suffering of leukaemia the first time. Would I have imagined that it will come again ten years after the first one, two years after full discharge from hospital appointments? No, I did not, and no one would have expected the same. That is the awesomeness of God and why He is omnipotent and Lord over all.

Having a stem cell transplant is also a life-changing experience. First issue was to deal with the uncertainty of the treatment and the impact of the treatment on my everyday life. I was already aware of possible emotional, physical, and financial issues I may experience after treatment if I survived. I have also found that not everyone around you will ever understand the level of emotions you feel for going through cancer treatment and stem cell transplantation.

Every cancer patient has their own unique ways of dealing with 'post-transplantation disorder' (*this is name I have coined for the purposes of this book to the experience*). I had to draw on God's grace and strength to see me through the difficult and uncertain times. I have gone through a life-changing experience of having new cells; I did not quite feel the same person I used to be which was a bit of a problem for me at first; I looked okay, and everyone around me may have assumed that I was back to my old self. Was I back to my old self pre-cancer? Did I have major emotional issues surrounding my experiences in the hospital? Did I have a silent fear of a reoccurrence? It is a 'Yes' to all these questions. I am human, after all. But it was only the grace of God that kept me going. I did not comprehend how big of a problem this was until people around me made me realise the negative effect my mood changes and mood swings were having on their own person. Four years after leaving hospital, the effects are not totally gone, but God pulled me through, and I have enjoyed the grace of his mercy all the way. Praise God.

Recounting an experience of fatigue-related illness which I suffered post-transplant is scary. Exactly forty-two days after I was discharged from the hospital, I was attending a New Year's Day meeting of my socio-cultural group in East London. The meeting had been ongoing for about an hour, we have had some food and drinks and there was quite a bit of banter going on. I laughed at a joke and, suddenly, I could not remember what happened; but I was told that I slumped on the lap of the person sitting next to me, collapsed and lost consciousness, passed out for some minutes. Thank God for the quick wit of those around me, who noticed that I was not in a good place, and quickly raised the alarm to get me back to life. I did not know what it was, but I continued to experience this symptom which was later confirmed to be a rare situation called 'Syncope'. According to the American Heart Association: *"Syncope is a temporary loss of consciousness usually related to insufficient blood flow to the brain. It is also called fainting or "passing out.", (and) most often occurs when blood pressure is too low (hypotension), and the heart does not pump enough oxygen to the brain.*

(https://www.heart.org/en/health-topics/arrhythmia/ symptoms-diagnosis--monitoring-of-arrhythmia/ syncope-fainting)

Getting back to work as a chartered accountant since discharge from clinic has been challenging and life changing experience. God has been good because I am now in a good place, having nearly overcome all the stresses and anxieties post-transplant, and nearly back to my old self. God always leaves space for thanksgiving, and I am a *Living Testimony* today because of His grace. *"I have told you all this so that you may have peace in me. In this world you will have many trials and sorrows. But take heart because I have overcome the world" (John 16: 33 NLT).*

Jesus promised his disciples his peace on earth, even amid storms. We take biblical assurances for granted even in daily lives. Consider times in your life when you have taken for granted assurances of God speaking to you. Yes, you heard him speak, but was it loud and clear enough? Were you determined to do your own thing? That was exactly what I did. Imagine me taking on a journey of travelling to Nigeria in February 2016, barely three months of leaving hospital after stem cell transplant operations. I am going to leave the graphic details of that story there. But that singular act of mistake nearly cost me my life. That journey was a nightmare that did not need to have happened.

I got to Nigeria and spent the nine days of my stay in Lagos, terribly ill and I had to stay in bed throughout the whole holiday period suffering from what I later discovered to be *severe pneumonia*. I was too scared to go to any hospital in Nigeria because I was not sure if it was safe to have other doctors attend to me who knew nothing about my medical history. By the time I got back to the United Kingdom, I was admitted back into hospital where I spent about nine days. I mentioned this, so you can ask yourself questions when you want to do your own thing and God is speaking to you. It is amazing to know that despite my stupidity in making that journey, against all reasonable advice from my wife and brother, God saved me. He was merciful to me through it all. He is merciful and full of compassion. Yes, he overcame the world for us all. Praise God.

MANAGING FATIGUE

At the initial stages of discharge from hospital, I wake up daily acting as though I had so much energy, but it was all a fluke, a front I put up for the benefit of the world. But who was I fooling? Did it make me feel better pretending to be "all-okay-Jack" kind of person? Have you ever thought that something you do or the personality you present can be to your disbenefit? What with the many types of medication that I had to contend with daily? I was taking an average of fifteen tablets three times a day, that is a total of forty-five tablets in one day. Just in one day!

But I had no choice because the medication kept me going, to maintain the process of growth of new cells, and to help prevent possible Graft Versus Host disease after transplant; generally, to keep me alive. When you are given such conditions as a necessity for you to take medicines, they are weighty enough reasons to comply. Managing fatigue after transplant is never easy because your body and your system have been altered through transplant, and unfortunately, the way you handle fatigue can be a burden on the family and they can be a burden to you, the patient.

It is true that families suffer when spouses, relatives or friends go through life threatening illness, but the sufferings differ between the patient and families. It is impossible to understand and feel what a cancer survivor feels post treatment; you cannot understand the trauma, the fear, the anxiety that the patient feels. I have read so many research papers because I thought I was the one with the problems when I started having depressive periods and mood swings. Neither did I understood why, or what I was going through. How would anyone around me understand what I probably do not even understand myself? But the best antidotes during these times is to focus on the positives around you. I felt that I was already in the situation I was in, and nothing was going to change that. Stressing about it was leading to fatigue and fatigue was leading to a depressive state. But I did not go as far as getting on anti-depressants because I had the fear that would be counterproductive. Motivational speeches which are genuinely meant to inspire are good but did not work all the time for the cancer survivor. You get people around you psyche you up and boosting your ego by saying things like: *"Hey, you are not the only one who had gone through cancer and survived it, so stop being miserable and cheer up."* This is where it is important for relatives to get greater understanding because chastisement is counterproductive. I had professional counselling, and it was good. Talking to a neutral person about your traumas outside of the family circle helps you to be open about things. I may never go back to the old me, but then who does? And what was the old me? Managing post-transplant fatigue taught me to speak affirmatives to my life through God's word. I constantly prayed Psalm 91 over my life, and it was reassuring to read in verse 5: *"You shall not be afraid of the terror by night, nor of the arrows that flies by day"*.

In managing fatigue and stress, I changed my circumstances by seeing me through Gods eyes. What will God do here? What does God see in my circumstances right now? So, it was a question of me making plans to get away from that state of being fatigued and depressed to a place where God has plans for me, where I can look to the future and dream that the contents of this book will bless lives and transform the mindset of people going through leukaemia or any form of cancer that *it is not unto death, it is not a death sentence!* Part of the plan should also include physical activities to allow free flow of blood through the veins, these are simple life rules that need not be told to anyone but believe me when I say though we know it, we need to be told again and again and again. I involved myself in light exercises, brisk walking was part of daily activities, I am not even sure I am doing a good job of that, hence the need for the emphasis of being told again and again and again. Pressure of life can sometimes make it difficult to prioritise your wellbeing and health, but seeing things through God's eyes, planning for them, and doing the best we can with what we have goes a long way to making life better after transplant.

"He who dwell in the secret place of the most high, shall abide under the shadow of the Almighty, I will say of the Lord he is my refuge and my Fortress; My God, in Him I will trust" Psalm 91: 1-2

CHAPTER 14
PAYING IT FORWARD

Finding myself in the position of a two-time leukaemia survivor made me more aware of my ignorance of many things that I take for granted hence I decided to be an advocate of cancer cure, to promote education and awareness, support cancer research through independent fund-raising projects, and to make a difference. I also needed to know more. Being an Accountant has been all I knew all my adult life: debits, credits, cash flows, budget, and preparation of client's financial statements under recommended accounting standards. This was just a means to an end, and the end has always been to make money, acquire position and have a comfortable life. But there is more to life than just making money because money is just a means of exchange for the good things of life. There is quite a lot to learn if we just look outside of the box where there is happiness everlasting, by impacting lives of those suffering from leukaemia and other ailments positively and helping them in their treatment journey. I sincerely hope that this book will fulfil that purpose as people read about the experiences of my own travails and victory during treatments. I decided to carry out some empirical research into the treatment of leukaemia as a prelude to setting up a foundation as a vehicle for that purpose first, and to understand how possible it was that I was afflicted with the same disease twice in ten years. It was no surprise that there is an abundance of resources online and there is no reason at all why anyone will pretend to be ignorant of knowledge of leukaemia or any type of cancer. Like most cancers, and despite the difficulty in the treatment of Acute Myeloid Leukaemia, there is evidence of good news.

At the first diagnosis for leukaemia, one of the most shocking revelation from doctors was that human being is born with cancer cells in our body system not everyone will get cancer. Evidently, some people live all their lives being careless with their health, having bad health habits, yet they live a long life without cancer ever developing. This is a mystery. Conversely, others live clean healthy lives, exercise, eat well, go on holidays, but could still be diagnosed with cancer. Treatment has advanced over the years allowing a greater percentage of people to survive leukaemia more than before. Information from Leukaemia and Lymphoma Society confirms that *"there has been a slow, but steady improvement in survival rates for patients with leukaemia and related diseases over the last 30 years. Much of this has occurred because of better prevention and management of problems such as infection and bleeding (Haemorrhage) and anaemia"*. It goes on to say that *"many of these aspects of treatment are similar in patients with different diseases. Acute Myeloid Leukaemia was reported to have 29.4 percent survival rates overall in 2018, whilst that figure was 68.7% for children and adolescents younger than 15 years"* (Facts and Statistics published by Leukaemia and Lymphoma Society in 2018). Figures from Cancer Research UK shows that about *71%* of men survive leukaemia (all subtypes combined) for at least one year, and this is predicted to fall to 54% surviving for five years or more, as shown by age-standardised net survival for patients diagnosed with leukaemia during 2010-2011 in England and Wales. Survival for women is slightly lower, with 66%. I am one of those 54% survivor as I am currently in remission five years after the relapse and stem cell transplant!

In the United States, there are about 345,422 people living with, or in remission from leukaemia (2017 figure). The overall five-year relative survival rate for leukaemia has more than quadrupled since 1960. From 1960 to 1963, the five-year relative survival rate among whites (only data available) with leukaemia was *14 percent*. (American Cancer Society). I was unable to find any comparable data for Nigeria or other African countries, probably due to lack of verifiable data available for those surviving. However, sadly, survival amongst ethnic minority groups is extremely low compared to white people.

Black people of African and Caribbean origin particularly have low survival rate from Acute Myeloid Leukaemia because there is a shortage of donors amongst this ethnic group for Stem Cell transplant treatment that patients need to survive. Stem Cell transplant (also called peripheral blood stem cell transplant) *"is a treatment to try to cure some types of cancer, such as leukaemia, lymphoma and myeloma. You have very high doses of chemotherapy, sometimes with whole body radiotherapy. This has a good chance of killing the cancer cells but also kills the stem cells in the bone marrow"* (Cancer Research UK). The reason for this situation is that there are very few blood donors amongst the Black and Asian ethnic groups, probably due to lack of awareness or lack of information regarding the procedure to donate.

My daughter was eight when I had my stem cell transplant, but she and my wife spent time with me at the accommodation the hospital provided. To my amazement, she can recount some of her experiences of sitting with me when I had my chemotherapy and seeing me suffer with pain. I asked her to do some research about cancer because she was asking me a lot of questions about the disease. Here below is the result of her desktop research, which I have graciously copied verbatim with no amendment except to check for spelling errors. I am sharing this because it is an inspiration for me that she showed an interest in knowing how things have evolved and how she can share her findings in her school projects if the opportunity comes up.

UK = info from Cancer Research UK

- Almost 4 in 10 (38%) of all new leukaemia cases in the UK are diagnosed in people aged 75 and over (2015-2017).
- Leukaemia is more common in White and Black males than in Asian males.
- Leukaemia is more common in White females than in Asian or Black females.
- Incidence rates for leukaemia in the UK are highest in people aged 85 to 89 (2015-2017).
- White males with leukaemia range from 12.3 to 12.9 per 100,000
- Black males are similar, ranging from 7.7 to 14.2 per 100,000
- Asian males are significantly lower, ranging from 6.3 to 10.6 per 100,000
- White females range from 7.3 to 7.7 per 100,000
- Asian and Black females are similar ranging from 4.1 to 7.3 per 100,000 and 4.7 to 8.9 per 100,000

USA – Info from American Cancer Society

- Between 2012 – 2016, 18.1 per 100,000 of leukaemia incidents in America were male; whilst 11 per 100,000 were female
- Whereas between 2013 to 2017, 8.6 per 100,000 deaths were male and 4.8 per 100,000 were female

- Breaking it down to race and ethnicity, 14.9 per 100,000 of leukaemia incidents were Non-Hispanic; 11.3 per 100,000 Hispanic White during 2012 – 2016
- Similarly, 11.1 per 100,000 leukaemia incidents were Non-Hispanic Black; 10.2 per 100,000 incidents were American Indian and Alaska Native; and 7.7 per 100,000 incidents were Asian and Pacific Islander in the same period of 2012-2016
- Regarding Leukaemia deaths, 6.8 per 100,000 were Non-Hispanic White; 5.5 per 100,000 Non-Hispanic Black; and 4 per 100,000 were American Indian and Alaska Native; all taken during the period 2013-2017
- Age Probability to developing cancer, taken between 2014 – 2016 ranges as follows:

  o From 0 to 49 years there is 0.2 percent of probability
  o 50 to 59 years there is 0.1 percent of probability
  o 60 to 69 years has 0.3 percent of probability
  o 70 + years has a 1.2 percent of probability

- Age probability ranges for those likely dying from cancer, also taken during the same period

  o From age 0 to 49 years there is >0.1 percent of probability
  o From age 50 to 59 years there is >0.1 percent of probability

- o From age 60 to 69 years there is 0.1 percent of probability
- o From 70 years upwards, a 0.8 percent of probability

Wow, she gathered information from *Cancer Research UK and American Cancer Society* which related for just about everyone, black people, white people, Hispanic and non-Hispanic. She did her research and I give her credit for providing the information. Thank you, my darling baby girl.

IT IS IMPORTANT TO DONATE BLOOD

The process of donating blood or stem cells are simple and have no significant side effects on the donor's health thereafter. Blood supplies in the UK for example, are obtained from unpaid volunteers who donate blood at regular intervals. Many patients with leukaemia and related diseases require blood transfusions at some stage during treatments, whilst some require stem cell transplant as the last resort. This is especially so when the person has an aggressive disease that requires treatment that stops the bone marrow from producing blood cells.

During my treatments at both Barnet Hospital and University College London Hospital, I regularly required blood transfusion which helped my blood circulation. I hope that by the time you read this book, many will understand the importance of donating blood. I am writing this section at a critical time when the entire world is experiencing a pandemic that we have never seen before, the Corona virus. It is amazing how many people responded to the call of the government and volunteered to support the National Health Service during this difficult time. In the same vein, there is always an appeal for blood donors every time. If you are healthy enough to donate, you might help to save a life. It does not have to take a pandemic for us to volunteer to donate blood because to donate is painless, to donate is human, to donate is doing our duty as Christians in alleviating the pressure on other patients whose only saving grace might be just the drop of blood you donate.

It is reassuring to see that survival rates for patients with leukaemia and related diseases have improved over the years. Continuous research has also enhanced and changed the methods of treatment for leukaemia and related diseases. For example, apart from blood transfusions to help patients to benefit more during treatment, other transfusion methods have been modified to be more effective for patients. Red Cell transfusion and Platelet transfusion have all been made more effective through continuous progress in medical research. Apart from this, early diagnosis significantly reduces the risk of death for leukaemia patients. Taking a precautionary approach to personal health is a reassuring way of preventing leukaemia or other related disease. Personal hygiene is essential because of what we eat, regular exercise, and careful consideration of hazardous things like smoking and drinking are effective and preventative measures against leukaemia and related diseases. Like everything in life, it is important to set some personal maintenance health goals, light exercises couple with daily activities, and observing rest periods help in preventing against unexpected leukaemia. It is important to know the body function by keeping an internal diary of what is best for one's health and how we set healing goals.

This book is not a medical journal, nor has it been written by an expert in blood cancer and related diseases. The contents of this book are my personal experiences which I hope will give an insight into a patient's view and experience of leukaemia. Knowing what I know now, I probably would have been a better patient when I was diagnosed. Talking about personal hygiene, the British Committee for Standards in Haematology state that *"Careful attention to hand washing and decontamination before contact with the patient is mandatory for all health care workers and visitors"*. The same is true for all of us. Cleaner environments, regular health check and regular exercises are all measures of preventing leukaemia. ***"PREVENTION IS BETTER THAN CURE."*** There is now an avalanche of information readily available online, so are organisations that provide resources, help and advice on prevention. Cancer Research UK, Macmillan

Cancer Support, University College Hospital Cancer Fund, Andrew Nolan Trust, African Caribbean Leukaemia Trust, and many others now provide resources and information on cancer prevention. It is important that the imbalance of blood donors and stem cell donors amongst the ethnic minority groups is corrected as there are many patients from this group who, at one time or the other, will require matching donors during their treatment.

Let us work together to fight cancer.

CHAPTER 15
PHOTOSPEAK

"I shall not die but live, to declare the glory of the Lord" Psalm 118:17

At this stage, I want to share with you some pictures during my treatment so you can appreciate the grace of God upon my life. Cancer is the most disfiguring disease I know. It manipulates the body structure and turns the patient into a completely different person. I sometimes look at myself these days and wondered if it really was me in those pictures. My whole-body structure changed, my skin colour changed, my face changed, and there was nothing about my appearances in these pictures that reflected me. I am sharing them for readers to appreciate that nothing is difficult for our God!

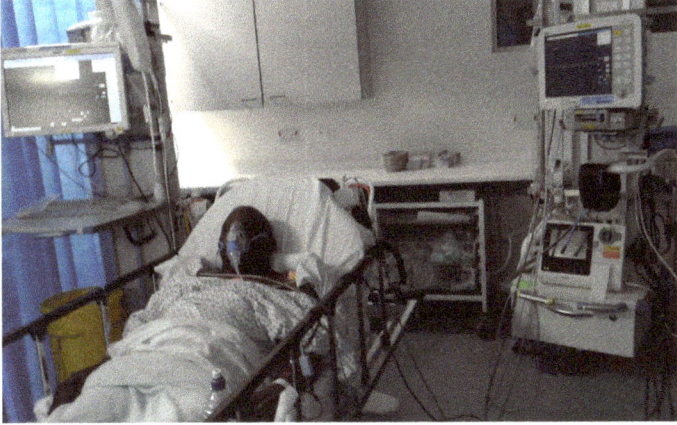

Pic 5: My life in His hands, God is great

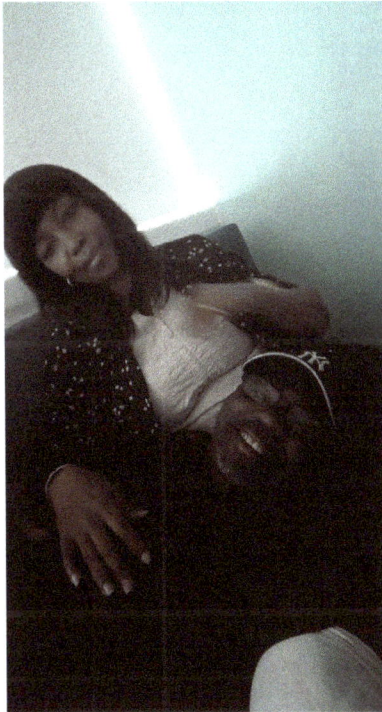

Pic 6: At difficult times like this, you need your family

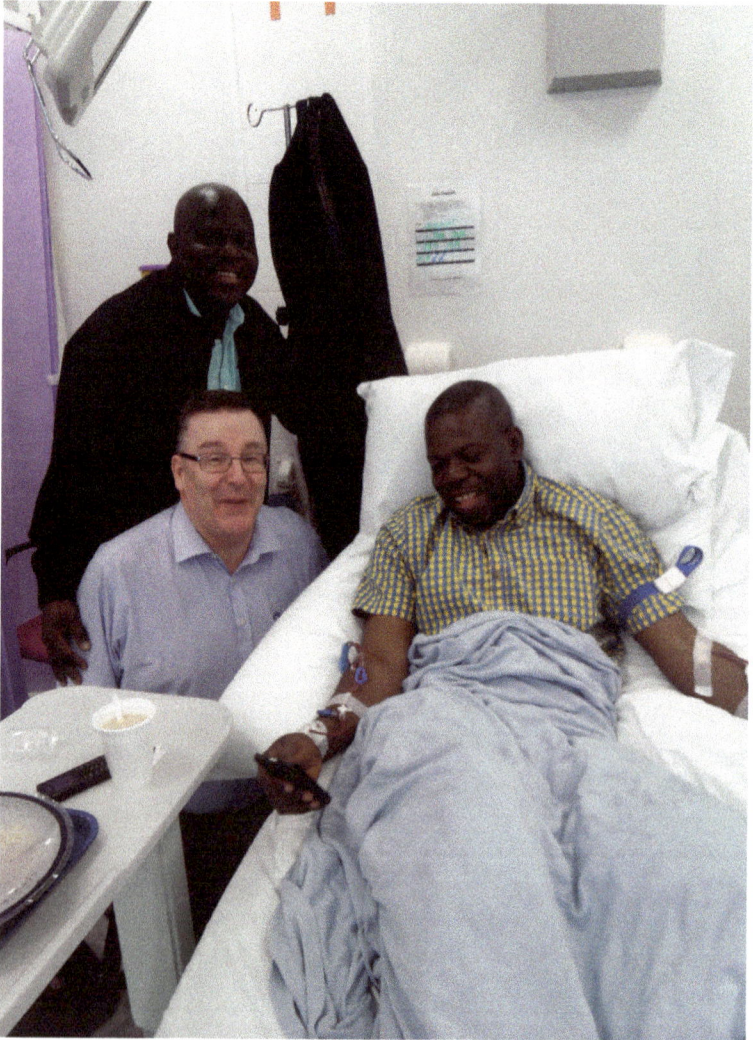

Pic 7: Pastor Phillip of LC Cuffley in attendance during cell donation

*Pic 8: Black as charcoal, effect of
chemotherapy darkened my skin*

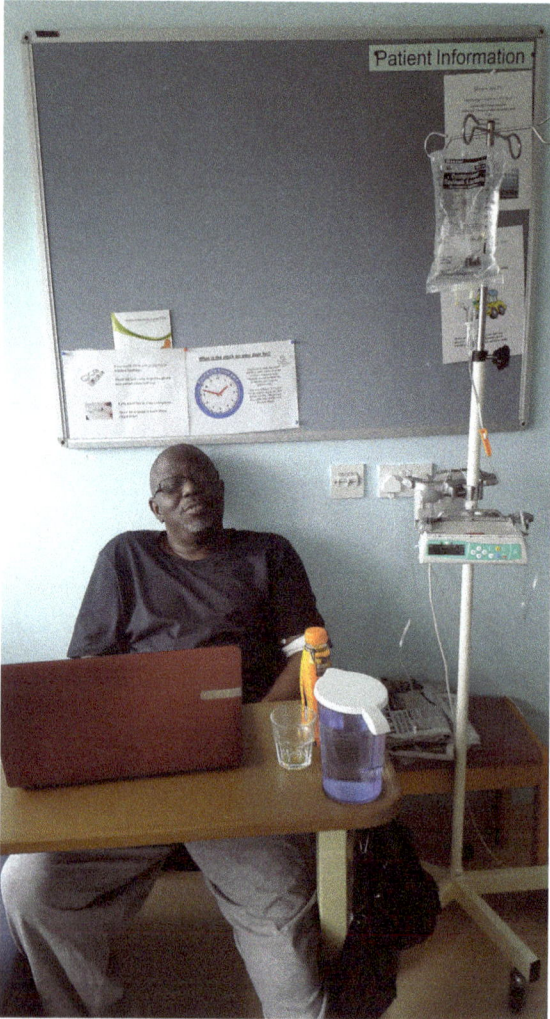

Pic 9: Lifeless, aged but hopeful at Cancer Centre

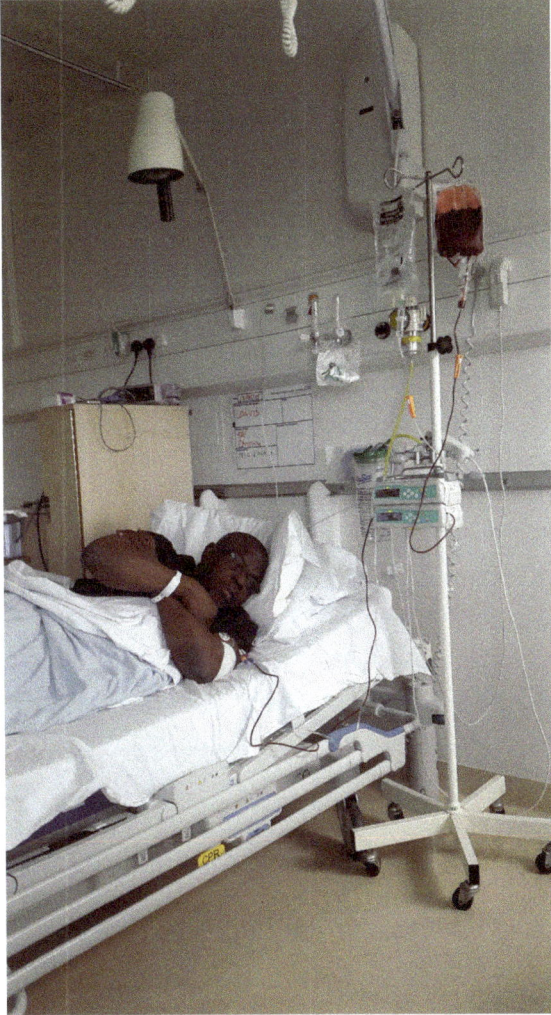

Pic 10: Sleeping was normal for me to forget my troubles. Praise God.

Pic 11: My first outing at Cancer Research UK office

Pic 12: It was all over, praise God. First holiday after Stem cell transplant at Welsh Assembly complex in Cardiff.

Pic 13: My first outing volunteering for Cancer Research UK
on the Road Show program! Praise God.

HEALTH AWARENESS VOLUNTEERS NEWSLETTER
EDITION THREE : 2016

So the summer seems to have finally arrived (and with it, increased numbers of questions about skin cancer) which has made being on the Roadshow a much more pleasant affair! I believe everyone has now been out and about with their team which is fantastic, I know the nurses and RLMs really appreciate you spending your time with them. In this edition of the newsletter we've got results ago go, some lovely photos and all sorts of updates from the Annual Review to a new Volunteer Advisory Panel. Let's get started!

Results so far

As of the 11th August, we had welcomed 32,150 people on board our Roadshows during the 2016 Campaign. This means we have reached over 30,000 people with our health messages, certainly no small feat! Specifically, you wonderful volunteers have:

Volunteered 268 hours of your time
Spoke to 1780 members of the public

60 Second Interview with...David

1) Why did you want to volunteer on the Cancer Awareness Roadshow?
I wanted to and did volunteer to serve on the Cancer Awareness Roadshow because after surviving Acute Myleod Leukaemia twice in the last ten years, I wanted to dedicate some of my time to volunteering for CRUK. I wanted to be part of the CAR program to help in creating awareness and education for potential patients, especially in my own ethnic minority group where there is acute shortage of information and cell donors.

2) What have you enjoyed the most since starting on the Roadshow?
I have enjoyed speaking to people and sharing my experiences when I felt it was necessary and required, but above all I have enjoyed sharing the good news of CRUK to bring information to every person, and to make people aware of the need to maintain a healthy lifestyle.

3) What have you been most surprised to learn whilst volunteering with us?
I have been most surprised with how little information there is available out there, despite efforts from organisations like CRUK and other Government agencies. I have also been surprised about people's negative attitude towards information about cancer.

4) Where in the world would you most like to visit?
Gosh, I will like to visit a lot of third world countries and, if possible, spread the gospel about cancer awareness. Having lived in the West for more than three decades, I will like to travel the length and breadth of Africa, South American countries and South East Asia.

5) What's your signature dish if cooking?
Honestly, I am not so good at cooking because my wife is the best cook in the world! But I can make a good Spanish Omelette!

6) What 3 things would you take to a desert island?
Plenty of drinking water
Sunglasses
Sun cream

Here is a sixty-second interview that I had with Cancer Research UK as a Volunteer on the Health Awareness Roadshow programme. Extracted from the HAV Newsletter for August 2016.

CHAPTER 16
A NEW SEASON

"To everything there is a season, A time for every purpose under heavens." Ecclesiastes 3: 1.

There were times as I have explained in this book that I did not know if I was going to be alive to write this testimonial. Then there were times I built up my hope during those heady days of treatment at the hospital as an in-patient, when it all looked bleak and my war against cancer seemed unwinnable! But then here comes the season of victory and testimony for by His Grace I have overcome. The truth is I am not sure how to conclude this book of my testimony because there is more to come, through the goodness of God in my life. Perhaps it is appropriate for me to thank everyone in the church family who, in one way or the other, were involved in my healing process through prayers, visiting, and phone calls, etc.

Although time has passed in the five years since I left hospital, I must not forget to appreciate God's goodness shown towards me through His people in those trying times. My greatest gratitude goes to Almighty God who spared my life and saved me and made it possible for me to be here to share my experiences in this book. I could not live without the Love of Jesus because that has been my tonic and wine in my time of distress, and my time of systematic healing by the Blood of Jesus. I thank God for belonging to the family of God within the Church family.

I consistently pray that the Lord will continue to enrich our Pastors and our leaders in the Christian family everywhere. I pray that God will endow these leaders with the Wisdom of Solomon to lead Gods' people in the right direction. Psalm 120: 1 says *"In my distress I cried to the Lord, and He heard me"*. This was so true throughout my treatment periods in both cases of my leukaemia experience. I had no choice but to keep crying to the Lord especially in moments that I did not know when I will come out from my darkest days in the hospital ward. God is truly omnipotent, a silent listener to His children in the days of trouble.

This is not an autobiography because that is another story entirely. It is about appreciating the grace of God upon my life specifically during my times of affliction with leukaemia cancer, and to encourage someone that may be going through some form of affliction or the other, that famous saying of Pastor Matthew Ashimolowo of the Kingsway International Christian Centre (KICC), that *"It is not over until God says it is over"*. Your affliction may not be like mine, it may not be leukaemia cancer, may not even relate to cancer at all, but it is the same antidote required to overcome.

We must believe in the power of God for deliverance and miraculous healing and holding on to His promises even when it makes little sense to do so. Quoting from the small book, *God's Creative Power for Healing* by Charles Capps, he said: *"Many today is seeking healing, yet they talk sicknesses and sufferings until they establish that image in them. Their thoughts and words produced a vivid blueprint, and they live within the bounds and limitations of that blueprint."* My message, testimonial and experiences shared in this book has focused on the following points:

- Health is wealth, and it is important to drive this point home especially to my male readers. I hasten to say that our womenfolk are more concerned about their health than most men, and it does not even African descent. We would rather spend our money on cars etc and forget to take care of our body with healthy eating, healthy lifestyle, regular physical body review, and work-life balance.
Social Network - by this I am talking about the fact that it is not just the cancer sufferer that is going through pain, immediate families are too. There is a need for understanding amongst families, friends, acquaintances and especially Church family to have complete understanding because no one can understand something except

they go through it. There is a need for greater awareness among the family of God because, unknowingly we may make comments that grieves the Holy Spirit because of our attitude towards issues we consider as to have resulted from the sufferer committing a sin. I remember the first time I was diagnosed, and a family friend came to visit me in hospital, bringing along with her a Pastor who I had never met before to come and pray for me to get healed. The idea was noble enough, and I appreciated it. But I remember the Pastor telling me that "I may have been afflicted with leukaemia because I committed sin, I was not praying to God or believing in Him enough" What a thing to say to someone facing one of the most horrible, life-changing disease? Not knowing if I was going to survive and then hearing that, it created doubt, but one needs to be physical and spiritually strong with a sound mind to overcome that kind of utterance, and by God's grace, I did.

- Faith is the evidence of things not seen but hoped for. Faith brings healing, Faith brings unmerited Grace of God to bear on us when trouble comes. It will not be easy, it may not be instant, the outcome may not even be as we want, but total faith in God and humbling of self before Him are expedient for His word to come through in our lives. *"Humble yourselves therefore under the mighty hands of God, that he may exalt you in due time" 1 Peter 5:6*

Last, but not least, I believe the battle is safely won and my victory is complete. I can safely brag about the manifold blessings and grace of God in my life that I am the only living soul I know who has survived Acute Myeloid Leukaemia cancer twice. Here I am now, a LIVING TESTIMONY, testifying to God's goodness of His grace upon my life, Hallelujah! The Bible confirms this when it said:

"Many are the afflictions of the righteous, But the Lord delivers him out of THEM all" (Ps 34:19). Note the word "THEM ALL" not some of them.

Say the following aloud on my behalf. *"The Stones the builders rejected, has become the Chief cornerstone. This is the Lords doing, and it is marvellous in our eyes"* (Psalm 118: 22 – 23) This Psalm has been my song always. Remember that help is always at hand. Remember also, that *'Together we will beat cancer.* (Cancer Research UK. The slogan used to be: *Together we are fighting cancer)'.* But we are no longer fighting cancer, together we will BEAT cancer! If you notice any of the symptoms described in this book happening to you or someone you know, please do not keep quiet about it. Pray, yes, but above all seek medical attention, get it checked out and get yourself medical treatment. I pray the Lord of hosts will direct and guide your thoughts and your minds always. Remain blessed in His name. Amen.

CHAPTER 17
PRAYERS FOR HEALING

Dear Father, I pray fervently that this book is a blessing to the reader. To those who read this book in their time of difficulties of going through cancer or any illness, please bring upon them your healing grace. Let them see you clearly in their time of need. I pray this in Jesus Mighty Name. Amen

Jesus, I thank you that you have both the power and authority to heal my body. I boldly come to you today to ask for your grace and healing power to be at work in my body. I trust that you are powerful and looking for an opportunity to show your power in my body. Cause this sickness to leave my body in Jesus' name. I break the power of stress and trauma and release your peace. I speak to every part of my body and say, "Be whole in Jesus' name." Function properly—the way God designed you to function Jesus, send your word and heal me today. You paid the price for my healing, so I trust that you are at work in me. Holy Spirit fill every part of me with your supernatural presence. Drive out all that is not good, holy, and true. I receive the healing you have for me today, in Jesus' name. Amen.

Thank you, Father, for sending Your Word to heal and deliver me from all destruction caused by Leukaemia or any kind of cancer. Jesus, You are the Word who became flesh and dwelt among us. You bore my pains and carried my sickness. You were pierced through for my transgressions and crushed for my iniquities. And by Your stripes I am healed completely. Amen

Since the Spirit of Him who raised Jesus from the dead dwells in me, He Who raised Christ You Lord, that I will prosper and be in health, even as my soul prospers. I am healed of this cancer completely, and I shall be a living testimony. Amen

Father, you are my heavenly Father. You have not given me a spirit of slavery that leads to fear, but you adopted me in your family. You created me to be your child, forming me in my mother's womb. What a great love you have for me. Before I was born, you had great plans for my life. Thank you, Father, for accepting me to your family. Today, I turn away from sin and choose to serve you as my heavenly Father and follow your Son, Jesus. I bless my own family. I forgive them for ways they did not exemplify your heart for me. Forgive me for not doing my part in having a family that honours you. Make things right in our relationship. Heal us and help us to be the family you want us to be. Amen

As in James 5: 15, "And the prayer of faith will raise him up. And if he has committed sins, he will be forgiven". Father, I confess my sins and claim my complete healing by the Your Word.

And we all say: AMEN.

Personalise these prayers for yourself and see God's miraculous healing upon you. I have experienced it, I am a *"Living Testimony"* to the mercies of God

ACKNOWLEDGEMENTS

My greatest appreciation goes to God Almighty who healed me of Acute Myeloid Leukaemia (AML) twice. He helped me grow my faith to withstand all the pains and sufferings of cancer treatment, and to come out victorious. So many people have played an important role in my life. If I do not mention you in this book, if I do not appreciate you here, I know God will reward you with manifold blessings for all you did for me, because that is God's promise. I would like to acknowledge the following people for all the emotional, physical, and spiritual support they gave me during days and months of going through treatment in hospital. I wish to appreciate all the medical personnel involved in my treatment on both occasions; Consultants, Doctors, Nurses and all the entire staff at the Haematology Wards at Barnet General Hospital; the University College London Hospital Haematology and the Bone Marrow Transplant Unit at Macmillan Cancer Centre. There are many people at both hospitals that deserve my appreciation, they are too many to mention. All I can say is THANK YOU. I am glad I made so many friends because I owe each person a bunch of gratitude for all their care.

I would like to appreciate my spiritual family at The Kings House Edmonton; The Apostolic Church Kennington, Life Church Cuffley especially Pastor Philip Coffin, Derek, and Mary Gregory. Phillip Coffin always found time within his busy pastoral duties to visit me regularly in University College London Hospital. I would also like to acknowledge Rev (Dr) Victor Akerele and the entire membership at First Baptist Church, Festac Town Lagos. They were my support system during my remission period between the first and second diagnosis.

My appreciation also goes to my friends who contributed one way or the other to help me through my two experiences. Dr Ayo and Lawunmi Adeyemi, Alistair Soyode, Dawnette Legister, Tunde & Funke Akiode, Kevwe and Toyin Yerifor, Tunde and Shade Omopariola, Akintunde and Toyin Seweje, Anthony and Joy Obisesan; Selina Adu, Christine Ogunkanmi, Taiwo and Nike Fakoya, and Captain (Rtd) Ibrahim and Wunmi Olugbade. My childhood friend, Dr Femi Fakolade, Comfort Wilson, Modupe Okeowo, Ike and Victoria Onu, Ian Harvey and Bridget Gbemudu-Harvey, and many others I could not possibly mention here. I bless God for all of you, and I thank you all. You all played a part in my treatment, and subsequent healing.

My in-laws, the Edomwonyi's, the Solankes, the Elegbas and the Onwordis. Dr Ima & Dr (Mrs) Nosa Edomwonyi, Francis Edomwonyi, and Andrew

Edomwonyi are all worthy of mention. And finally, let me appreciate my family who stood solidly behind me throughout. My brother (best in the world that anyone can have for a brother), Adekunle Oladipo Fadipe and his wife Ololade; and my sister Foluso, who came to spend time with me during my first treatment. My brother's sacrifice to donate his cells for the much-needed transplant operation during my second diagnosis is substantial, without which I may not be here to write this book.

My dear wife, Helen Adesuwa was a constant rock of physical and prayer support, without which I probably would not have made it to the finishing line of healing. My jewel-in-the-crown of a daughter, Elizabeth Eniola, was and continues to be exceptional. Although she was at a tender age of eight (8) when I was admitted to hospital for my second cancer treatment, it was amazing how caring and concerned she was for my health at such a young age. I appreciate all these wonderful people that God has blessed me with as my friends and family. God said in 2 Sam 12:12 *"You did it in secret, but I do this thing in broad daylight before all Israel".* All your deeds for me in secret will be rewarded openly in Jesus Name.

Thank you all and God bless

REFERENCES

Capps, C., 1991. *God's creative power for healing.* Harrison House.

Copeland Germaine, 2001. *Prayers that avail much for the workplace.* Harrison House

Hunter, J. (2016). *Prayers and Promises for Healing.* Broadstreet Publishing Group LLC

Hunter, M., 2001. *Strong Medicine: Prescriptions for Successful Living.* Whitaker House

Osborn, T.L., 1983. *One Hundred Divine Healing Facts.* Destiny Image Publishers.

"The author also gratefully acknowledges reference materials from the following organisations:

Leukaemia and Lymphoma Society in 2018

Cancer Research UK Newsletter articles

American Cancer Society Journal articles

Cancer Research UK; Macmillan Cancer Centre; University College Hospital Cancer Fund; American Cancer Society

Society of Cancer Research Organisation of Nigeria (SOCRON)."

Lightning Source UK Ltd.
Milton Keynes UK
UKHW020204230621
385972UK00001B/1

9 781839 755552